"I've read hundreds of books on speaking. Many of them are very much the same, but there are some intriguing ideas in this book that set it apart from all others. One is the importance of connecting with your audience. Connecting is the magic that ties the audience to the message. I encourage you to read this delightful, informative, and exciting book!"

Terrence J. McCann, Executive Director
Toastmasters International

"Margaret Hope has managed to do in print what she does so well on the platform ... and what the readers of this book are enabled to do – connect with an audience! With an abundance of good sense advice and a superabundance of personal stories, she keeps her readers turning the pages in eager anticipation of the next great idea, illustrated by the next great story from life. You will love this book, written by someone who loves and lives the platform."

William D. Thompson, Ph.D.,
Author of Speaking for Profit and Pleasure: Making the Platform Work for You,
General Editor of The Essence of Public Speaking Library, General Editor

"I wish I'd been exposed to this approach to speaking much earlier in my career. Margaret Hope's book is down-to-earth, practical, and an entertaining read. It is chalk-full of real life examples – each chapter concludes with concise bullet points."

Gayle Stewart, Vice President Corporate Communications
at a major telecommunications firm

"'You're Speaking, But Are You Connecting?' is a terrific book, and belongs on the bookshelf of everybody who has ever dreaded giving a speech, or wondered how to be a more effective speaker."

Anne Fisher, "Ask Annie"
career-advice columnist, Fortune Magazine

YOU'RE SPEAKING –
BUT ARE YOU CONNECTING?

by Margaret Hope

First published in 1998
Reprinted 2000, 2004

Lions Gate Training Ltd.

Tel: 604-320-7613
Fax: 604-320-1660

email: mhope@lionsgate.ca
www.lionsgatetraining.com

10 9   8   7   6   5   4   3   2

Canadian Cataloguing in Publication Data

Hope, Margaret Fern, 1952-

You're speaking—but are you connecting?

Includes bibliographical references.
ISBN 0-9683973-0-1

1. Public speaking.   I. Title.

PN4121.H66 1998   808.5'1   C98-910665-9

The author has, to her knowledge, credited anyone quoted, paraphrased or referred to. In the unlikely event that anyone was missed the author gratefully acknowledges their contribution as well.

Project Manager: Heidi LeRossignol of Behind the Book Production Services
Editor: Patryce M. Kidd
Cover deisgn: Anne Dunnett of Inklings Design Studio
Back cover photo: Dave Roels
Text design: Ruth Linka

Distributed in Canada by Sandhill Book Marketing Ltd.
Orderline: 1-800-667-3848
Fax: 250-763-4051
email: sandhill@direct.ca

Printed and bound in Canada by Webcom Limited

DEDICATION

Dedication: to my husband Carl Vanderspek — without his love, respect and support this book would not have been written.

ACKNOWLEDGMENTS

First to my success team who have encouraged and challenged me: Jan Miko, Dave Howard, Melissa Tharp, Lori Vanderspek, and Kathy Lynn. When I lost enthusiasm you reminded me of my dreams, when I lost courage you shored-up my resolve, and when I complained you listened and then told me to get on with writing it. Thanks!

Thanks also to my other dear friends and my many colleagues who always seem to care about my projects and insist I complete them, notably: Judith Dawson, Kristi Nielsen, Dawn Miller, Tanis Helliwell, Gwen Ellert and Judy Denham.

I also want to thank those who read and commented on my book: Ian and Sally Wilson, Melissa Tharp, Terry McCann, Gayle Stewart, Melissa Hope, Lori Vanderspek, and William D. Thompson. Yours was the greatest commitment of time and effort. Your suggestions refined my ideas and my writing and your encouraging words helped me complete this book.

To Heidi LeRossignol at Behind the Book for her professionalism, encouragement and wise suggestions. Your team of dedicated professionals were amazing: Patryce Kidd for her editing, and Anne Dunnett for cover design and Ruth Linka for text design.

A special thanks to those who agreed to have their stories and experiences told: Morgan MacAthur, Judy Johnson, Doug Anderson, Paul Sickler, John Nichols, and Terri Dickneider.

Finally, my thanks to the two people I most count on for love and inspiration: my mother, Marion Hope, and my husband, Carl Vanderspek. Thanks for believing in me.

TABLE OF CONTENTS

Section Three: Tools for Connecting

Section Four: Strategies for Connecting

Perhaps THE BEST WAY TO START THIS BOOK IS TO TALK A LITTLE ABOUT how it is different from what other writers have said about speeches and presentations. As you read their work, you'll notice their many specific instructions to speakers. They tell you how to stand, where to put your hands, what kind of notes to use, and how to structure your speech. They are less likely to tell you why you should follow their instructions. And while much of their advice is helpful, it can't possibly work in every speaking situation.

As I write this book, I want you to understand that I do not believe I can give you one right answer to cover all, or even most situations you will face as a speaker. Instead, it is my goal to help you think about your presentations in a way that will help you make wise choices. And, as the title suggests, those choices should always be based on audience needs so that you don't simply give a speech or deliver a presentation, but, most importantly, you connect with your listener.

Other writers certainly advise you to learn about your audience, and many give suggestions regarding the use of information you gather during the audience analysis stage. This is where most writers leave the subject of audience analysis – as a step in the speech creation process. But it is far more than one step in the process. As you will learn from this book, it is an element of every decision you will make in planning, creating, selecting audio and visual tools, delivering your speech, handling audience interaction, and even in interacting with your audience before and after you speak.

I want to stress that, in order to connect, every speech must be customized to the unique needs and interests of your audience. Speakers often insist this is impossible with large audiences, yet I've seen speakers create intimacy and an emotional bond with huge audiences. In this book you'll learn how to create that connection with audiences large and small, using a wide range of tools and skills.

There are four sections to this book. In Section One, connecting is defined and you'll learn why it is so important. In Section Two, you'll learn how to accumulate audience knowledge and how to apply your knowledge as you easily map out your speech or presentation. Section Three introduces a wide range of techniques you can add to almost any presentation to draw you nearer your audience. Section Four examines the delivery process and gives tips in a chronological manner for assuring maximum audience connection before, during, and after you present. Following each chapter, I've provided a brief summary of the main points, and the final chapter of the book offers a review of the key concepts for connecting.

SECTION ONE: CONNECTING IS THE GOAL

CHAPTER 1

WHY CONNECTING MATTERS

SUPPOSE YOU WERE ASKED TO SPEAK TO A GROUP WHO ALL WISHED TO BE entrepreneurs and, following conventional advice, you'd spent time learning about their interests. The adviser for their program told you to expect forty students who were skilled computer users and suggested you prepare an on-line computer slide presentation. But, when you went to deliver your presentation, if you found only four participants, would you still follow your plan? If you followed the advice in most speaking textbooks, you would use your visual presentation as you had planned. Does this seem like a good idea?

In my opinion, you would have missed a phenomenal opportunity to connect with your listeners and make a change in their lives. With only four people, you could learn their names and entrepreneurial plans, and you could adjust your remarks to include information they'd given you. You could customize your presentation to meet their needs.

You could also alter your presentation if, at the last minute, several additional classes joined in and your presentation was moved to a huge gymnasium where the equipment for your on-line presentation wasn't suitable. In this situation, you could wander about the audience while they were settling in and find out what interests they have, or you could devote a few moments at the start to talk with the entire group and get suggestions of key ideas they'd like you to cover. Without the benefit of your visuals you'd find other ways to illustrate the speech, perhaps relying more heavily on stories, examples, and interaction with your audience. You know far more about your topic than you could ever put into a speech, so why not use the opportunity to connect with your audience even if it means abandoning some or all of your planned speech?

The approach I'm recommending has some definite advantages for both the speaker and the audience. It is far more personal and engaging for your listeners, so they are inclined to stay attentive and recall more of what you've said. They interact with you as you speak and allow you to continually adjust your material to meet their needs. They are then more likely to be persuaded to agree with you and support your ideas.

But this isn't just about the audience; it's also about you, the speaker. With the approach I'm recommending, you'll see better results and feel intrinsically rewarded. You'll find this approach far easier than slavishly following the rules and advice offered in more traditional texts on the subject of public speaking. Best of all, you'll enjoy it more.

THERE IS ALWAYS A WAY TO CONNECT

I frequently speak to groups about networking, and I always emphasize the need to create a bond or connection when first conversing with a potential contact. I believe you can create this bond with almost anyone if you think about their interests and needs rather than your own. Ironically, the following story happened as I was on my way to deliver my networking speech at an international convention in New Orleans.

My husband accompanied me to the convention and we hailed a cab at the airport. As we headed to our hotel, I noticed some lovely flowering trees along the highway and asked our driver about them. I was warming up for my speech by attempting to connect with a stranger. He responded with as few words as possible telling me that, yes, those were flowers and someone had planted them and he didn't know anymore about them. I assumed our driver didn't wish to have a conversation with us, but I was wrong.

My husband then asked him how many miles he had on his odometer. It was as if a key had been turned in a rusty lock and the door slowly but surely opened. After telling us he had 1.2 million miles on the odometer, he entered readily into a discussion of servicing and caring for his geriatric vehicle, and from there into how many hours he worked and how his schedule compared with other cab drivers. The conversation moved from taxi licensing to his city, his family, and his philosophy of life. We learned he'd sent his children away for higher education and jobs believing they'd achieve more away from a community he considered dangerous for young people. He sadly told how his many nieces and nephews who had remained in the area had each spent time in prisons and how determined he was to keep his children and grandchildren from a similar fate. All this information and a delightful conversation simply because my husband asked the right question. He had connected with the cab driver, while I had not.

This experience made an excellent opening to my speech because it perfectly illustrated my point; you can create a bond with almost anyone if you think about their interests and needs rather than your own. And this generality applies to speakers as well as to conversationalists and networkers. No matter what situation you are in, no matter who you are addressing, there is a way to connect with others. There is a way to gain their attention and their interest so they will tell you what you need to know and thus help you communicate effectively.

In my example, a simple question connected one person to another. You've likely had many similar experiences, so you know how good it feels to connect in conversation with another human. But is it possible to create the same wonderful feeling when you are speaking before a group? The answer is yes, and I will help you do just that as you read on.

WHY DOES CONNECTING MATTER?

Before I show you how to really connect with an audience, I need to answer a crucial question, one I'm often asked by the many speakers I teach and coach. They ask, *"Why does it matter if I connect when I'm just making a speech or presentation? Isn't it enough to have a smooth, well-prepared presentation, one that delivers the information they need?"* What they are really asking is, *"Why should I change?"* The answer can be found in one word, communication.

Communication isn't merely about someone talking and someone listening. Diagrams of communication theory show information travelling from a sender to a receiver and simultaneously from the receiver back to the sender. These models show that communication flows in both directions with both speaker and audience involved in the process of giving and receiving information.

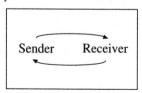

Figure 1: Communication Cycle

If you deliver a speech or presentation, one you've carefully crafted and then committed to memory and rehearsed for dramatic delivery, and you deliver it as planned, your mind will be on your carefully crafted, memorized, rehearsed presentation. Your focus will be on content and flawless performance when you should be focused on your audience. If you are like most speakers, the results will seem adequate, but won't come even close to the goal of communicating with your listeners because you are sending your message, but you aren't simultaneously receiving their messages. You are talking, but you aren't truly connecting with your audience.

WHY CONNECT? BECAUSE YOU ARE SELLING!

Another way to answer the question, *"Why does it matter if I connect when I'm just making a speech or presentation?"* is to consider why you are making the speech or presentation. The answer, with rare exceptions, is because you have something to sell. Some speakers are actually selling a product or a service. When my insurance agent presents, he wants me to purchase additional life insurance. Many speakers are selling an idea or a concept. A speaker asking her executive team to approve continued funding of a research project is selling a concept. Whether selling a product, service, idea or concept, all speakers have something less tangible to offer. They are always selling themselves. Selling themselves as credible, reliable individuals worthy of the trust and respect of their audiences. So, every speaker has something to sell.

In order to sell yourself, your products, services, and ideas, you need to win the support of your audience, the buyer. How does that buyer make a decision? Is it purely based on the logic and clarity of your ideas? It might be, but it rarely is. Based on surveys of executive-level audiences, conducted as research for his book, *Talking to the Top,* Ray Anthony[1] described how high-level audiences make decisions. Senior executives admitted they were far less persuaded by the content of the presentation than by the passion or deep belief a speaker was able to convey.

This passion isn't a measurable attribute. It's a feeling the listener gets. Something in the way the speaker talked made the audience feel his or her conviction and respond to it. The speaker connected his or her ideas and beliefs to those of the listeners who were, in turn, engaged by the presentation and completed the communication cycle by giving cues, both verbally and nonverbally, that they were engaged. Had the speaker simply planned and executed a near perfect performance without this connection, the sale would not have been made.

Because you will always have something to sell when you speak to others, you must connect with them. When that connection has occurred, when that chemistry is present, your audience will listen attentively, believe you, and if you've done your homework, will buy what you have to sell.

WHY CONNECT? BECAUSE IT FEELS GREAT!

There is a third way to look at this question, *"Why does it matter if I connect when I'm just making a speech or presentation?"* You have learned that real communication and buying decisions occur when your audience connects with you. The most compelling reason for connecting, however, is far more personal, and perhaps even selfish.

Speaking in public is a challenge and can be terrifying if the audience, the situation, or your purpose make your presentation seem especially critical. When you learn to connect with the audience, you'll suddenly find speaking far easier, more rewarding, enjoyable, and quite possibly exciting and slightly addictive. Where once you might have given presentations only because they were required, you'll gradually find yourself offering to speak and lead others publicly, and you'll observe how much you are enjoying the act of communication. Connecting simply feels better because it is true communication; it allows you make the sale by winning the attention and support of your listeners, and it uses skills you already have.

As you read through the following chapters, you'll be amazed by how simple the suggestions are. In fact, you've probably used many of these techniques in ordinary conversation without thinking of them as speaking skills. But somehow, when you were asked to deliver a speech or make a presentation, you discarded the very techniques that would most help you connect.

Eye contact provides an excellent example of this. Most of us use quite a bit of eye contact in simple conversation. Our eye contact helps us connect or form a bond with others involved in the discussion. We see their reactions to our words and adjust our communication to these reactions. By contrast, many speakers faced with the more formal public speaking or presentation situation, in an effort to ensure a perfect delivery, rely heavily on speaker notes and visuals and find it difficult to really make eye contact with an audience. These speakers know that eye contact is helpful in their conversations, and most of them probably know it would be helpful in their more formalized communication opportunities. Yet faced with that larger audience, they ignore their own internal wisdom and proceed without the benefit of eye contact.

USE YOUR EXISTING SKILLS TO CONNECT

So, if you are like many of the speakers I've worked with in the past two decades, and you feel more relaxed and effective during informal communications than you do when faced with a more formal speech or presentation, you already have a great many of the skills you need to connect with an audience. I'll show you how to adapt those skills to more formalized speaking situations. In fact, communications can be placed on a continuum (Figure 2), and as you read through this text you'll notice how skills used at the informal end of the scale are readily adapted for use with larger audiences and more formal speaking.

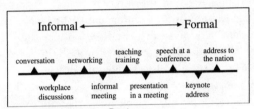

Figure 2: Communication Continuum

Whether simply conversing, leading a meeting or discussion, making a presentation, or delivering a formal speech such as you might at a conference or in addressing a large public audience, you can connect with your listeners and get the results you need and want.

SUMMARY: WHY CONNECTING MATTERS

- There is always a way to connect — you can reach any audience.
- You must connect to communicate — otherwise you're just speaking.
- You always have something to sell and you must connect to sell it.
- You'll get better results and enjoy speaking more when you connect.

Notes

[1] Anthony, Ray. *Talking to the Top.* Prentice Hall, Inc., Englewood Cliffs, NJ, 1995.

SECTION TWO: THE BASICS OF CONNECTING

CHAPTER 2

AUDIENCE KNOWLEDGE – THE KEY TO CONNECTING

THE PLACE WAS SOUTH AFRICA, THE AUDIENCE WAS INTERNATIONAL, THE organization was Young Presidents, and I was in the audience to witness one of our first speakers repeatedly refer to us as, *"you Americans."* I was surprised, the Korean gentleman seated next to me seemed perplexed, and the Dutch woman seated next to him, after hearing the assumption for the third time, quietly said, *"I am not an American."* Later on, an American speaker said, *"here in America we have…",* and later, *"we all live in a country with many freedoms."* Where had these speakers gotten their audience information? Even if they hadn't done their homework, a quick look around would tell them they weren't back home in Kansas and the audience didn't all hold American passports. Knowledge of your audience is the first step in connecting.

You can't open a locked door without the key and you can't connect with your audience if you don't know who they are. In almost every text on public speaking, presentation skills, negotiation, and interpersonal communication, you'll be told to learn about your audience. Despite this advice in some very good texts, I believe speakers rarely take the time to do enough audience research and when they do, seldom take advantage of all they've learned.

Perhaps this is because texts suggest learning about the audience but rarely show speakers that audience analysis is not something done in a few minutes at some point in speech preparation, but rather is an ongoing process of investigation. Audience analysis begins the moment you accept a speaking engagement and finishes with your final contact. Let's look at an example of a typical business situation.

AUDIENCE ANALYSIS – AN ONGOING EXPERIENCE

Someone walks into your office and asks you to address a client group who will be there later in the afternoon. Of course you'll be speaking about a topic you know well; you aren't being asked to invent a speech. You are the expert or they wouldn't be asking you. What you need to know at that moment is who is the client, who will be there, what are they expecting, and what, of all you know, will be most useful to this audience in fulfilling your objective? You also need to know details as to where the client group is meeting and how long they'll want to listen to you.

Let's assume for a moment that the request came from a senior partner in your firm and was relayed by his assistant, Dan. You'd ask Dan what he knows about the client, probably talk to the senior partner to learn more about the players, and then get into the files on this client to learn a little more about their business dealings and relationship with your firm. Next, you'd get on the phone and speak with someone at the client firm, learn who will be in the audience and something about their specialties or interests in attending your presentation. In some cases, you'd go even further and speak to several others from the client group.

If you learned that Elizabeth, a co-worker from another department of your firm, spoke to their management team a few weeks ago, you'd put in a call to her. She could give you advice about their attitudes and behaviour. You could ask her about the types of questions they asked, about their willingness to interact, about their reactions to her material, and about any concerns she thinks they might want to discuss. Elizabeth could tell you of any participant who seemed difficult or hostile. Just because someone was tough on Elizabeth, or supportive of her, doesn't mean you'll get a similar reaction, but you'll often find there are trends and similarities.

Armed with this kind of information about your listeners, you'd organize your remarks, gather any visual support, and perhaps take some time for a dry run or rehearsal. You'd arrive early to set up and thereby be ready when the client group arrived. As much as you could, you'd match names to faces and gather additional detail. This period of socializing would help set you at ease, give you additional audience knowledge, and begin the process of connecting.

As you spoke, noticing a reaction from a listener to something you said, you'd pause and enter into discussion with the group. Once that point was resolved, you'd return to your planned presentation but with additional knowledge about the interests of your audience. As each question was raised, you'd respond using the name of the person who asked it. And when you presented your planned remarks, you'd indicate if certain information might be of special interest to one or more of the group. With this style of speaking, the interaction, and therefore your ability to continue to gather audience knowledge and adjust your remarks, would be ongoing. With your rapport with the group well developed, there would be several more personal discussions following your speech and likely some follow-up by phone.

In this hypothetical example, your audience analysis began as soon as you knew you would speak, and it continued until your final contact with the group. If you addressed them on several occasions, this analysis would be cumulative. Despite what you've read or seen other speakers do, if you want to truly communicate with your audience, you'll make this process of learning about them an intensive, ongoing focus.

AUDIENCE ANALYSIS STRATEGY #1: PHONE YOUR AUDIENCE

Let's look at some examples of how various audience analysis strategies pay off. I often recommend speakers contact one or more members of their audience by phone before the speech. It takes time but, as you'll see in this example, it is very rewarding and can be influential in their evaluation of you.

I once had a woman approach me after my speech to tell me what my phone call had done for her. She was the department head for Occupational and Physical Therapy of a large hospital, and when she heard about the topic of my presentation, putting pizzazz into hospital training, she was sure it would be a waste of time. In her words, *"Been there, Done that!"* Of course, I didn't know this was her attitude when I called her prior to the session, but I remember she was reserved and quite negative at first, gradually becoming more fluid and relaxed as we spoke. Eventually she offered me some fine examples of problems she'd encountered and overcome. I chose one of them for my opening story and made a second call to her to get permission to use the story. This time she was far more enthusiastic in her response and said she looked forward to meeting me and had decided to bring several people with her from her department.

While visiting with me after the presentation, she described her attitude and told me how my calls had altered her opinion of the session. Best of all, she told me she'd learned something valuable from my session and planned to invite me to her facility to work with her entire department. She did and I've been back several times to work with various departments in that hospital.

I have no idea how often what I've described happens, but I do know that each phone call, in addition to providing essential research, is an opportunity to change attitudes and beliefs. I also know that what we do, our behaviour, is as important as any content. If you can encourage participants to come to your program, and if you can raise their curiosity or pique their interest before they arrive, your presentation will have far greater impact.

AUDIENCE ANALYSIS STRATEGY #2: PHONE PREVIOUS SPEAKERS

I not only talk to participants, I also like to talk to someone else who has addressed the group. Of course this isn't always possible, but in many cases it is. In my university teaching I am often asked to speak as part of a team of instructors. Cumulatively, we teach management skills, but no single instructor is responsible for all topics. Someone teaches behavioural management, someone handles finance, someone teaches how to write business proposals, and just before the end of the program, I teach students how to present their proposals before a board of directors. I always talk to several of the instructors who precede me and have many times been given excellent advice.

A couple of years ago, we had a class that was outspoken and highly critical of any information or activity that seemed to them impractical or a waste of time. Several instructors commented on the situation, so I felt it was a trend. They gave me two helpful pieces of information. One, they provided me with examples of situations where participants were critical, which helped me to determine what content and methods I'd use. Two, they identified three participants who seemed especially reactive and mentioned their leadership role in the group.

Although I don't usually contact many students in this program, I made sure I phoned those three. I asked them about the program so far, about their knowledge of my topic, and about their work, and got some excellent examples of situations they'd already faced. I even learned that two of them dreaded making presentations while the third considered himself an expert. As it turned out, he was a strong, confident speaker who participated well in my class by taking the role of expert.

I made a point of introducing myself to these three students before the class started, and I used examples from our phone calls during the early parts of the class. At the first break, one of them came over to talk, telling me it was the best class in the series (for him) and giving me the best example of all. Their non-verbal reactions, participation, and general friendliness told me I'd connected long before I had a chance to confirm their opinions on the course evaluation. In this situation, my fellow instructors gave me the essential information to make good decisions about how I would teach this class and who was most important to contact. Don't overlook the value of other speakers who have addressed the group. Turn their problems into your opportunities.

Sometimes a previous speaker will let you know what a great audience you'll be facing. Once I was asked to speak to a tourism organization at dawn on a Friday. I'm not, by nature, a morning person and I didn't really expect the majority of the audience would be either. Although I'd agreed to speak, I certainly wasn't feeling enthusiastic about the task, and the woman who called me, a hired administrative assistant with the organization, gave me little information and no encouragement. She refused to give me contacts but said she'd tell the president to call me. No call had come, my speaking date was drawing near, and I was feeling anxious. So you can imagine my relief when a co-worker identified a chap who had addressed the group only a month before. I made contact with him and was rewarded with wonderful, revealing stories about the group I was to address. He told of their humour, their interaction, and their upbeat mood. He also gave me business cards from several participants so I could begin to make calls. The group was every bit as impressive as he'd described, and I had a terrific time because he gave me the information I needed.

One participant, the owner of a Bavarian restaurant, arrived wearing leather shorts (lederhosen). He asked me a very funny question about the meaning of a certain female communication pattern. He didn't really expect an answer and was obviously used to having fun with the speaker and his fellow members. My contact had mentioned a similar experience with a fellow dressed in lederhosen. I responded to his question with about the same degree of levity as he displayed and made some comment about the communication impact of men in leather. I still meet people some twelve years later who say, *"You talked to our group once and weren't you the one who did the thing about leather shorts?"* I'm not sure they remember everything I told them that morning, but I do know I connected with this group. I became one of them by entering into their world, something I could not have done without the advice of my co-worker.

AUDIENCE ANALYSIS STRATEGY #3: TALK TO GATEKEEPERS

A third technique that yields a great deal of advice about my audience requires another phone call or sometimes a site visit. If I'm going to do a seminar or program for a company, I'll often talk to a gatekeeper. Gatekeepers are the folks who answer phones, handle reception desks, and serve as assistants to the people I'm going to address. They are deserving of much respect and will usually be very helpful if you take time to learn their names, find out their affiliations and interests, and treat them with dignity. The following story illustrates just how valuable these gatekeepers can be.

I'd had a brief call from the partner of a prestigious investment firm. I'll call him Mr. Wharton. He had a deep voice, a very formal style, was spare with his words and, although he booked a two-day program for his firm, I got the feeling he had little interest in the project. Subsequent calls were succinct, businesslike, and at times almost cold. It was very difficult to get any phone time at all with him. I really needed to know more about his interests and background because he planned to join the session with eleven of his juniors.

In preparing for the session, I often spoke with his assistant Grace and found her pleasant, warm, and helpful. Finally I asked her for a bit of information about her boss, Mr. Wharton. *"Oh, Warty? He's really a great guy. He's very supportive and well-liked by everyone. He'll help you make the sessions successful, and I know he's very pleased you've agreed to speak."*

I was stunned. My first response was, *"Warty? You call Mr. Wharton, Warty?"* She confirmed that everyone did and proceeded to give me additional information about his business skills, his style, and his ability to become part of the group. Armed with this surprising information, I felt more relaxed about the program and in my communication with *"Warty,"* although I never called him that. The sessions went fine and I have Grace, a gatekeeper, to thank for her timely and valuable input.

Never overlook the value of a gatekeeper in doing your audience research. Various assistants have sent me corporate videos, reports, and brochures, and offered to help in any way they could with details. They've offered me additional contacts and tracked down the folks I needed to talk to. They've offered their own advice and observations, and solved problems I encountered with individuals at their firm. Best of all, they've often been the friendly face I met when I arrived. Gatekeepers aren't always part of your audience, but they are a vital part of the support team that can help you successfully connect with your audience.

AUDIENCE ANALYSIS STRATEGY #4: ARRIVE EARLY AND CRUISE

Arrive early, and once you've set up your materials and taken time for personal hygiene, cruise through your audience to gain last minute ideas. Whether you meet them in the refreshment area or visit with them as they take their seats, you can learn a great deal about your audience by asking why they are attending your presentation.

While waiting to conduct a negotiation seminar in Whitehorse, Yukon, I began to chat with a member of my audience, the owner of a floral shop. She soon told me how timely my seminar was; she was about to negotiate with her landlord who wanted to raise the rent on her shop. Her case, because it related directly to the local business scene, was better than any I could have invented. With her permission, we used it for discussion, and the audience gave her superb ideas on handling the negotiation. They were engaged and enthusiastic throughout the seminar, making my job easy and rewarding. One week later the florist reported a successful negotiation; thanks to the group she'd arranged a reduction in rent and several important concessions. I'm guessing the landlord wished he'd attended the seminar.

Although these are unusual tangible results gained by taking time to visit with an audience before a speech, they do reinforce my point. Audience analysis starts well before you speak but continues throughout your speaking engagement. Taking time to visit with participants and hear their reasons for attending your session can help you find excellent examples to add to your planned remarks. It can also alert you to problems and challenges that could lie ahead.

Visiting with one audience just before speaking to them, I learned that their general manager, someone they clearly cared about, was in the hospital awaiting the unexpectedly early birth of her first child. Because it was a premature baby, I couldn't have learned about its imminent arrival in earlier contact with the organizing team and a sample of participants. This was information I could only get by cruising through my audience as they arrived and listening to their chatter.

They were apologetic because due to their anticipation of the birth, they weren't as interested in my material as they ought to be. I was able to arrange regular maternity updates for the group, and thus assured, they were more able to settle in. When that baby was safely delivered about noon, we broke into spontaneous cheering and took a break while flowers were ordered and various individuals composed themselves. In this situation, I was able to adjust for my audience because I'd done my ongoing audience analysis.

The previous examples have shown how important it is to contact participants, former speakers, and gatekeepers in doing your audience research. You've also seen how important it is to keep doing audience research after you arrive to give your speech. The following chapter looks at some of the questions you'll want to discuss when you call or meet with these people.

Summary: Audience knowledge – The key to connecting

- Begin as soon as you know you will speak and continue until all contact with the client is completed.
- Ask the person who calls you for basic audience information.
- Find out who else to call: actual participants, sample participants, and others who have addressed the group or worked with them closely.
- Build relationships with gatekeepers.
- Read or view public relations material if it's available.
- Arrive early so you can converse informally with participants before your presentation.
- Interact during your presentation so you continue to learn about your audience.
- Remain after your speech to continue building the relationship and gathering information just in case they invite you to speak again.
- Recognize that audience analysis is an ongoing and cumulative experience.

CHAPTER 3

AUDIENCE KNOWLEDGE –
WHAT TO ASK

W HEN I WORK WITH SPEAKERS PREPARING FOR A SPECIFIC SPEECH, I'M amazed how few know even the most basic information about their audiences such as the size of the group and the length of time they expect to listen. There are certain pieces of information you'll want regardless of your topic or objective, but you'll also need to cultivate your own list of questions for each type of speaking you do. In this section, we'll first examine generic information and then some examples of specialized lists for distinctive speaking opportunities.

WHO WILL BE ATTENDING?

This is a huge topic, but at first all you really need to know is a general description. Information such as: *"they'll mostly be physicians," "we expect our Board of Directors and a few department heads," "students in their final year of Engineering Sciences,"* or even, *"it's a complete cross-section of our community,"* gives you a starting point for further analysis.

When I'm told a group will be mostly anything, I try to learn who the exceptions will be. A wood products firm I was working with told me to expect, *"mostly our sales force,"* but on closer investigation I learned that nearly half the group members weren't in the sales force and had quite a different perspective on the topic of teamwork. It was already a case of them-and-us, sales people versus non-sales people, so I especially needed to gear my speech to deal with the differences in their perspectives.

WHY ARE THEY ATTENDING?

Ask this question early and often. Try to find out if they need or want the information you're offering and if so, for what purposes. Sometimes they just want you; your topic is secondary. Peter Legge,[1] a popular motivational speaker, is a good example. I've heard him give the keynote address at five conferences in the last few years, and he always manages to lift my spirits. I doubt that his audiences ask about topic; instead, I expect they want results. So find out if your audience wants to be motivated, if they want to learn, or if they want to be challenged with new information. Sometimes, such as with service clubs, they meet regularly and always include a speaker as part of their program, but their primary purpose is fellowship. And, if you have more than one type of participant within an audience, such as I did with the wood products firm, take into account that they might be attending for different reasons and learn what those differences are.

ARE THEY ATTENDING BY CHOICE?

Sometimes it is apparent that groups are assembling either by their own choice or at the command of others, but it isn't always obvious and you'll often have a mix. Most conference groups attend of their own volition, but some may have been told by their sponsor to be at your session. When you offer training seminars, you are likely to have some (or all) participants there as a requirement. Most executive groups are there because it is a requirement of their work, but they are also likely to be highly motivated and won't regard themselves as being forced to attend. Community groups, service clubs, and public programs usually attract those who want to attend, while a class of ninth graders will feel more like prisoners.

The attitude of your listeners, their degree of interest, enthusiasm, and willingness to participate are all influenced by how much freedom they have to attend your session. If everyone in your group is there by decree and they can't see the point in what you're going to speak about, you need to work on selling your message. You've got to find out what they do care about and why they don't want to hear you, and then work to create a bridge.

I frequently teach undergraduate students in Applied Sciences. My students are predominantly male, 17- 21 years old, exceptional in math and sciences but not very interested in learning public speaking. Attendance in my course is required so they are truly like prisoners. The first time I addressed such a class, they sat slumped in theater seats, doing other homework and generally telling me non-verbally how foolish I was to bother them with such nonsense. They taught me a lot.

I now keep the session lively with plenty of humour and stories. To make it relevant, I use examples from the businesses they'll work in after graduation. To add urgency, I remind them frequently of upcoming speech assignments. I greet them personally as they arrive in the theater. I tease latecomers and sometimes make them perform before their peers, and I encourage a lot of interaction despite the limitations of the setting. I have a lot of fun with this group and still manage to convey some important life skills.

How do I know I'm getting results? Part of my feedback comes from colleagues at the university who tell me their students' presentations have improved, and some comes from students and former students. While speaking at a firm where many of our graduates seek work, a former student approached me to say how useful my course had been. He admitted he'd thought it was unimportant at the time, but now that he was in the real world he was regularly using the skills he'd learned. I appreciated the positive feedback and realized my adaptations for this highly specialized group were paying off. Knowing why people are attending helps you to decide how to adapt your ideas and information to help your audiences listen, remember, and believe your message.

How many people will attend?

The size of your group affects decisions such as room layout, audio visual aids, handout materials, the style of your presentation, and what additional audience analysis you'll be doing. If you learn you will have fifteen participants for your two-day seminar, you know you can encourage a high degree of interaction, use almost any type of visual, do without a microphone, and phone all or a large portion of the participants if you like. At a conference, you might be told there will be more than 500 delegates and that you'll be one of three speakers each in a room with a seating capacity of 200. You won't be calling 200 delegates even if you could determine who will attend your session, but you can arrange to speak with a sample of registrants, and you can plan to use elaborate visuals.

How long will they listen?

You might think of this question as *how long should I talk?*, but it isn't exactly the same. Successful business presenters often find their sessions go overtime because, although they concluded within the given time, they've aroused such interest that the group entertained an extension. But if you know your group has a deadline (for example, they all have to be on a bus to the airport thirty minutes after you start speaking), you'll know you need to plan a briefer speech so time is available for interaction and questions at the end.

Having a tighter speech pays off if your available time is suddenly reduced. Luncheon speakers, for example, are often asked to prepare a fifteen-minute speech but then find they get only eight or ten minutes because other activities take longer than planned, and the group leaves at 1:15 p.m. even if the speaker isn't finished talking. Because you never want to be surprised by a time limit, nor offend your audience by exceeding the allotted time, you need to find out how long they'll listen.

Depending on your style, you could have other reasons to ask this question. If you enjoy questions and discussion throughout your session, you'll want to know the total time available and warn the host that you'll take questions throughout and will therefore not save time at the end for them. If you are a seminar speaker used to doing several days of speaking, the answer to *how long they'll listen* is really about pacing the day. Can they listen for ninety minutes before they'll need a break? With knowledge of the time constraints of the total program, you can politely observe them and thus keep everyone comfortable.

What else is on their agenda?

Sometimes your audience has assembled just to hear you, but frequently you are only one part of a larger program. Additional agenda items can cause delays and time restrictions, they can alter the mood and concerns of the audience, and they can result in competition for the attention of the group. A client of mine was asked to speak for the final thirty minutes before lunch in a four-hour morning program. By the time they reached her address, they were already a few minutes late for lunch, but the group's leader went ahead and introduced her anyway. I felt my client made a good decision by telling the group she would adjust her presentation to twelve minutes, making them only fifteen minutes late for lunch, and offering to take questions informally throughout the luncheon period. Knowing your presentation is scheduled at the end of a heavy program, you can be prepared, as my client obviously was, to adjust the length and style of your session.

Mood and audience focus can also be altered by the events preceding your presentation. I spoke to a group of women employed in industries such as heavy duty equipment operation, construction trades, and sawmill operations; industries where relatively few women are employed. I'd spoken to this group before and found them receptive and eager, not in any way hostile about their working conditions. The speaker before me had addressed the challenges women face in working at non-traditional jobs and made some strong remarks about how men have traditionally kept women out of highly paid jobs of this type. She repeatedly gave examples of how badly women are treated in the workforce and how men drive women away, even now, from the very jobs these women have managed to secure. By the time I stood to speak they were angry about men in general, wanted to tell their own stories of mistreatment, and focused many of their questions on differences between male and female communication patterns. This didn't entirely catch me unprepared because once I knew the preceding topic and the speaker, I made a point of arriving early to hear part of her message. I witnessed her effect on my audience and knew before I began speaking that I'd have to adjust my presentation to their present mood. I didn't create the mood, but I did get to adjust for it.

Another consideration when your speech is but one part of a full program is competition. If you're slated to speak until 3 p.m. and the golf tournament is scheduled to start at 2 p.m., you can be reasonably sure some of your audience will be slipping out early to play golf. If an enormous beer-drinking competition is planned for the evening preceding your presentation, and you are scheduled to speak at the 7 a.m. breakfast, you can be sure some of your audience will be late and some won't be feeling top-notch. If you know your program overlaps or competes with another event or activity, you need to plan around this conflict.

I was scheduled to speak just before the first full video conference of a major telecommunications firm. Even though the small group of executives were highly motivated, they were also anxious about the upcoming session. I finally wrapped up my program early and spent the last half-hour working through their questions about communicating on television. This was truly *just-in-time* training. It wasn't what the organizer had requested, but since they weren't getting a lot from my planned session, adjusting for their immediate needs made perfect sense.

Has this group any contentious issues or unusual concerns?

Often, when I probe a bit, I learn that the group is under some sort of pressure or has an unusual concern at this time. Sometimes I can use their current interest simply to make conversation and show them I'm interested in their world, which I truly am. Sometimes I can work their concern into my speech as an example, illustration, or point of discussion. Sometimes I simply refer to it, sympathizing with their preoccupation, and suggest they let me know if they need unusual breaks to take calls or manage the issue.

On the first morning of a session on improving community relations, one group of employees in a large transportation firm learned layoffs were imminent. Some feared they'd lose their jobs, some worried about friends, and all were concerned about how the work would get done with a depleted workforce. With the approval of the training manager, I ignored my planned presentation for nearly thirty minutes while they discussed and absorbed the news. Then I worked through the topic, but wherever possible I included the relevance of the skills to job search and to rebuilding internal relations if and when the firm downsized. The program wasn't what I'd planned but we did cope with the unexpected circumstances.

A few days later the training manager phoned to thank me for being so flexible. Her department had been eliminated, but thanks to my presentation she already had two interviews lined up. When bad things happen to some or all of your audience, you need to adapt and provide leadership to help them adjust to whatever has happened, even if it means abandoning all or part of your planned remarks.

Where will my presentation take place?

The facility you will speak at is part of your audience analysis because this space influences group behaviour and such factors as your audio-visual aids. If the room is too large, you need to group furniture to move participants closer together for acoustic reasons and social factors. If the room is small, you need to consider removing tables, plants, and any other space-wasters.

Another behaviour influenced in part by where the presentation is held is audience readiness. Participants often arrive at the last minute, or even late, if the program is held in their own building.

They may still be awaiting a call or have even instructed an assistant to interrupt for an important message. The greater the distance from their offices, the more likely they are to arrive on time and return promptly from breaks. Presentations made at tourist facilities such as a casino, golf resort, or attractive shopping area might be an exception for some participants. Speakers who work on cruise ships claim they get far better attendance when the ship isn't in port.

In Chapters 11 and 12 there are many suggestions about adapting your speaking space, but most importantly, you need to know if the room is suitable for your visuals. Many public facilities have pillars, low ceilings, or vast windows that make projected visuals virtually useless. Speaking in the afternoon at a conference in Seattle, I waited until after lunch to view my meeting space. I wished I'd looked earlier because it was the longest, narrowest room imaginable and, with a low ceiling, I couldn't raise my screen enough for the back rows to see my visuals. Fortunately, my handout material contained snapshot versions of the slides, but had I done my homework, I would have requested multiple television screens at intervals along the room.

How do I get to my audience?

Once the setting is established, ask for arrival details. A client from a town about two hours away arrived at my office, exactly on time, bearing a highlighted map of the area and written details of how to find me. My office isn't easily located and he hadn't asked for details, so I asked who had prepared the map and written the directions. He explained his assistant always gave him such precise directions. Then I asked how she was able to give such directions and learned she'd spent time with my assistant to get the details she needed.

I wished I'd arranged for similar assistance when asked to speak at a local technology school with five downtown campuses. I lost thirty minutes of valuable time because I parked at the wrong facility. I arrived only ten minutes before my program was to begin and was preoccupied with thoughts that my car would be towed because I wasn't in an acceptable parking space.

Depending on your style and the situation, you might need to learn about travel and accommodations, exact location, traffic, and parking. When you work with the host to gather this information, explain that it's important to you to arrive ahead of time for set-up so you can be ready to greet participants. Your focus on the audience will impress them.

Summary: Audience Knowledge – What to Ask

• Find out what types of participants are expected.

• Learn about their interests, needs, concerns, and current challenges.

• Determine their motives for attending.

• Ask how many participants are expected.

• Ascertain how your presentation fits into their total program.

• Gather information about location and facility.

Notes

[1] Peter Legge is President/CEO of Canada Wide Magazines & Communications Ltd. He is a Toastmasters International Golden Gavel recipient and a National Speakers Association Certified Speaking Professional.

CHAPTER 4

CAREFUL SPEECH PREPARATION HELPS YOU CONNECT

THROUGHOUT THIS BOOK I URGE YOU TO FOCUS ON YOUR AUDIENCE more than your speech. Please don't think it's all right, though, to speak without having anything of value to say. I've heard a few speakers who were such showmen they could captivate an audience yet give nothing of value, but they are rare and few of us could or should aspire to such fraud. If someone pays you the compliment of asking you to speak, you need to carefully consider what you'll say. You need a message supported by sufficient structure to help your audience follow and understand what you are saying.

But traditional speechwriting methods don't result in presentations that are easy to deliver or readily adapted to audience needs and immediate circumstances. This chapter will give you suggestions on planning your presentation for an audience-focused delivery. You can save a lot of time and energy by planning in this way, and you'll also find it easier to deliver a speech without worrying about your exact words. Your delivery will improve dramatically with this system of speech planning.

I have assumed throughout this chapter that you speak about the topics on which you are an expert. Most of us do. If you are an orthopaedic surgeon with skull collecting and deep sea fishing as hobbies, I've assumed you'll speak about some aspect of orthopaedics, skulls, or fish. If your topic is, for some reason new to you, you might have to do some research. You would also have to do a lot more rehearsal with a researched topic since you wouldn't have extensive experience and accumulated knowledge to rely on. You might even decide to use a script, but it wouldn't produce an audience-focused speech, and it would reduce your likelihood of connecting with your listeners.

There are times when you'll need a scripted speech,[1] in which case you can use the following suggestions to quickly develop a draft version and can later polish your script or pass it on to a professional speechwriter for enhancements. If you happen to be speaking as part of a team, your team can use these suggestions to prepare the overall presentation, and individuals can work on their part following the same general procedures.

NECESSITY IS THE MOTHER OF INVENTION

I first came across this simplified and efficient planning tool while teaching. I worked with five teachers planning curriculum for 120 children aged six to twelve. We'd select a theme and develop curriculum around it, a process that occurred over several days in small bites of time snatched whenever we could. We'd first take huge sheets of paper and start mapping out our plans. Any idea given was recorded, no matter how silly or impractical, because often the silly or impractical ideas led us to the valuable or workable ones.

Other than theme and objectives, there were no limitations on what could be recorded. If someone thought of a resource person who could assist, the name was recorded; if someone remembered a suitable science activity, the activity was recorded; if someone had an idea for decoration or artwork, that too was recorded because we wanted to let our imaginations soar before we worried about structure.

Between planning sessions our brains seemed to continue to produce ideas without much conscious effort, so the map often grew even when we weren't formally meeting. As the plan grew larger, we'd put our efforts into editing and organizing. Eventually, individuals began to take responsibility for various parts and a final plan was recorded. It was always an enjoyable activity, and we created the best curriculum I'd ever seen.

It was also a flexible curriculum. If, at the last minute, a resource person became available, or budget for a field trip was approved, we were able to adjust to take advantage of the opportunities. If a group of students became engrossed in some aspect of the study and went far deeper into it than we'd expected, we could allow for their interest and excitement, capitalizing on the teachable moments as they presented themselves. Our planning process was flexible, but it was also easy. It made good use of our time and it got results.

I began to plan my own speeches using the mapping system and enjoyed the efficiency, the creativity, and the flexibility of the resulting presentation. I was further pleased by how much of the speech I could recall with very little rehearsal and no memorization. About ten years after I'd learned and adapted this mapping technique for my own purposes, I had the good fortune to meet author and speaker, Tony Buzan,[2] who introduced me to "Mind Mapping" and helped me understand why the process was so effective. If you're interested in more details of why a mapping system helps, I'd certainly recommend his books.[3] In addition, you might read Gelb's book[4] which gives a summary of the subject relative to speech preparation.

MAPPING YOUR SPEECH

Think of the first stage of planning a presentation as *dumping*. Simply dump whatever ideas come to mind onto your paper. If you haven't yet determined your *objective* or goal for speaking, you'll need to pause at this stage to figure out exactly what it is you want to accomplish; otherwise, you'll likely waste a lot of time on the subsequent steps. Once you're clear on your objective(s), you're ready to engage in stage two, *gathering,* where your ideas become more focused on the topics and main points you want to discuss. Gradually you'll start an *organizing* and *editing* stage where you determine the order of your presentation, eliminate material that's substandard or off topic, and *plan transitions* between your points. Finally you'll do some *rehearsal,* and if necessary, use your map to create visuals and notes. Let's look at each stage of the mapping process.

For the purposes of this examination we'll need an example. We'll prepare a simple sales speech for a totally fictitious product, the Tech-Chop'r. Imagine a product capable of reducing all household and garden waste to compost. It won't get rid of unwanted guests, but it will handle pet hair, worn out jeans, leftover breakfast, unwelcome garden pests, and homework assignments with equal enthusiasm.

DUMPING

I call the first stage *dumping* because it describes an effortless unloading of thoughts and ideas. As soon as you know you're going to speak, and you have a nascent idea of your audience, you'll likely find your

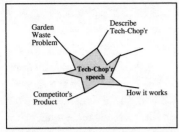

Figure 3: Dump ideas out randomly as they occur to you.

mind is flooded with ideas. Even if you have only a trickle of ideas, record them on a large piece of paper as soon as they present themselves (Figure 3). Don't edit your ideas and don't chastise yourself if some of your ideas are wild and seemingly useless. They might lead to great ideas later, so for now, just jot down any and all ideas. I strongly recommend you do this using plenty of paper so that as additional ideas come to you, you can give them their own space or cluster them near related ideas. By jotting down your ideas from the earliest moments of planning your speech, you'll be able to let your subconscious mind go to work for you.

CLARIFYING YOUR OBJECTIVE

Ideally you'd identify your objective first so all your thoughts would be focused on specific outcomes. But if you haven't already figured out exactly what your objective or purpose is, take time to do it now. Think of your objective in terms of audience needs. If you are successful in your speech, what will the audience think, do, or feel? When you say, *"My objective is to teach them to use the Tech-Chop'r."*, you are using a speaker-focused objective. When you say, *"If I am successful every participant will be able to use the Tech-Chop'r."*, you are using an audience-focused objective statement. The audience-focused statement is better because it describes the outcome rather than what you'll be doing. *"I want to sell ten Tech-Chop'rs."*, is a speaker-focused statement while *"If I am successful, ten people will buy a Tech-Chop'r."*, describes the results. You can almost always write a good audience-focused objective by finishing the statement, *"If I am successful my audience will..."*

If I am successful my audience will...

GATHERING

So, you've clarified your objective and you likely have some main points or key ideas randomly dumped on your paper. Now you're going to do some intensive audience research (Chapters 2 & 3), and with audience in mind, gradually gather appropriate stories, facts, and examples to illustrate those points. You've quite naturally moved from dumping to a more focused stage which I call *gathering*. You are consciously seeking ideas, points, information, illustrations, and examples to suit your audience and objectives (Figure 4). Record them all, even if later on you'll reject some and adapt others. You don't want to edit too early because you're still learning about your audience.

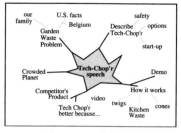

Figure 4: Gather additional ideas, stories, and facts of interest to this audience.

This is an excellent stage to involve others in the gathering and sorting of ideas. Talk to a colleague, friend, or coach[5] for help in fleshing out your ideas and fully developing your options. You can't edit and select the best if there are no options on your paper. Talk through your ideas to see where gaps exist and material is thin or too dense. If you have lots of time, work away at this gathering stage in brief sessions interspersed with more audience research and discussions with your chosen resource people.

ORGANIZING AND EDITING

If time isn't on your side, or you've used a lot of your available time for dumping and gathering, you now need to create some order from

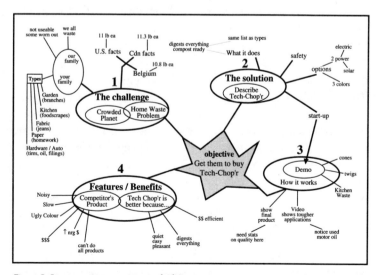

Figure 5: Structure starts to appear and editing occurs.

your chaos. Sometimes your main points will seem to leap off the page and logically arrange themselves. In that case you can just circle them and put numbers on each cluster to represent the order of delivery (Figure 5). Use lines and additional highlighting to link illustrations, quotes, facts, stories, and visuals to the key points you identified. If your points aren't cooperative, use a pencil to highlight and link related ideas until you have three, four, or five main points at most. You might need to rename several points to group them under one category, or you might want to delete some points that now seem unimportant. Eventually you need to bring order to your points even if you alter that order just before or during the speech.

MAKING TRANSITIONS

Once you have a rough order determined, talk through your points and work on *transitions*. A transition statement usually shows the relationship between the points. In moving from the first to the second point in our mythical speech about the Tech-Chop'r, you could say, *"You know the challenges we face as citizens of an overcrowded planet – and you know we need solutions. I have one for you today. Let's look at ... (speaker pulls off a cover revealing the machine) ... Tech-Chop'r."* Between points two and three the transition could be: *"I've given you a description of the Tech-Chop'r, but I'm sure you'll also want to see it actually work."* To shift from the third point to the fourth you could say, *"Now that you've seen how easily Tech-Chop'r reduces garden wastes into compostable form, let me review its advantages over all competitors."* From the transition statements you can determine the main points. Transitions are like road signs; they label each turn or change of direction in the speech.

It's amazing how quickly you can create your speech using only this map, now numbered, highlighted, and with transitions created. Through these steps, you've created the body of your presentation. You've identified the main points and arranged them in order, and you've selected from your map the subpoints and supporting matter to create a speech for this very specific audience. You haven't prepared an entire speech because you still need to put an opening and a closing on it, but you have done nearly all the required work. For details of those finishing steps, and a description of your options, refer to Chapters 13 and 15.

AVOID SCRIPTING IF YOU WANT TO CONNECT

At this stage some speakers like to create a more formal outline or a script of their speech. If you need a scripted speech for reasons mentioned earlier, writing will be your next step. But, for most purposes, scripting a speech is generally a time-waster. The resulting writing won't sound a lot like you should sound when you talk to your audience. In writing, we toil over constructing complete, complex sentences; in speaking, we simplify the words, shorten the phrases, and use repetition. And once you've created the script, you'll find it hard to deviate from it, so you'll have to read the text or memorize it. This results in canned, boring speeches that in no way fulfill the needs of the speakers or the audience because they do not connect.

REHEARSAL HELPS YOU CONNECT

A better use of your time is oral rehearsal. Speak from your messy map (or create a cleaner version to work from) in a conversational manner. Imagine your audience seated in front of you and talk to them as if they were there. If you haven't much time, do one rehearsal at full speed and then a second one at a slower pace with full delivery of pauses and vocal expression. Your goal is to become familiar with the pattern of ideas and main points in your speech, so a glance at your map or notes will help you move from one point to the next in a conversational way. Whatever you do, don't let yourself read from your script or memorize your points. Everything in this book is geared to helping you communicate. Reading or reciting to your audience won't help you do that. You'll do far better by referring to your map occasionally.

Also, at this stage, you can make visual aids which can serve as a memory aid if you create them properly. Don't make the mistake of trying to put your entire speech on visuals. They should serve as aids, not as a written version of your speech. Keep your visual material simple and learn to paraphrase it as you present.

For further tips on creating and using visual aids to enhance your relationship with your audience, see Chapter 10. For additional assistance, I recommend Ray Anthony's book, *Talking to the Top,*[6] which has a good chapter on using electronic visual aids, or Claudyne Wilder's, *The Presentations Kit,*[7] for illustrations and suggestions on creating visuals.

This has been a very brief summary on the process of speech preparation because it really isn't a complex process in most cases. I think speakers sometimes use the speech creation process as a form of procrastination. Perhaps they think, *"as long as I keep writing and researching I won't have time to worry about the actual performance."* But the performance, the interaction with your listener, is the only reason to appear. If it was just a matter of having a perfectly written speech, why not mail it to your audience so they can read it at their leisure? Unless your speech is going to be published or quoted, keep it very fluid by writing very little. The whole point of most speaking is to communicate, and that means you must be present, you must be conscious, you must interact with your audience, and you must connect. Connect whatever you plan to say to their needs and interests so they will listen to you, believe you, and do as you suggest.

In the following section you'll learn many ways to personalize the speech to the audience, and in the final section you'll see how the delivery itself can help you connect.

SUMMARY: SPEECH PREPARATION

- Start planning as soon as you know you have a speech to deliver.
- Immediately dump out your ideas on a large piece of paper.
- Clarify your objective once you've begun to understand the audience.
- Gather additional ideas and content (stories, examples, illustrations).
- Organize your ideas in a logical sequence.
- Plan transitions to connect one idea to the next.
- Use oral rehearsal to quickly build fluency and comfort.
- Create visuals to support you.
- Keep audience needs your priority and be prepared to deviate from your plan if that's what it takes to connect with the listener.

Notes

[1] You need a scripted speech if it will be published or quoted. If you are delivering politically sensitive material and an error would be embarrassing or expensive, a script can keep you out of trouble. For example, the Minister of Finance for a province or country should not deliver a budget speech without a complete script. If it is later published, excerpted for television and radio, and portions are quoted in various media, the Minister can't afford to speak in approximations lest she or he give inappropriate information on a highly sensitive subject.

[2] Tony Buzan delivered several presentations to the Young Presidents Organization, Mexico City, November 1996.

[3] Buzan, Tony. *Use Both Sides Of Your Brain.* Penguin Books, New York, 1991.

[4] Gelb, Michael J. *Present Yourself!* Jalmar Press, Rolling Hills, CA, 1988.

[5] Many speakers work with a speech coach to both create their speeches and work on delivery. A good coach will offer ideas, force you to articulate yours more clearly, ask for details and examples, and challenge material you've included. You might have a friend who can provide this service or hire a professional speech coach.

[6] Anthony, Ray. *Talking to the Top.* Prentice Hall, Inc., Englewood Cliffs, NJ, 1995.

[7] Wilder, Claudyne. *The Presentations Kit.* John Wiley & Sons, New York, 1994.

SECTION THREE: TOOLS FOR CONNECTING

CHAPTER 5

USE STORIES TO CONNECT

LET'S ASSUME FOR A MOMENT YOU'VE ACCEPTED A SPEAKING ENGAGE-ment, and following the suggestions in the first part of this book, you've begun to understand your audience. Although you haven't yet got a speech, you do have a rough idea of your objective and key points. You want those points to come alive for your audience. You want them to pay attention, remember your ideas, and perhaps take specific actions based on them. Maybe you want the audience to enjoy themselves and remember your name in connection with the good feelings your speech creates. This section of the book will show you how to use a variety of tools to make your points impressive, noteworthy, and even entertaining.

STORIES CONNECT US

When information is boring to an audience, you aren't connecting. Regardless of your message, if you connect it in a meaningful way to your listeners, they will stay attentive and be influenced by it. Stories are one of the many tools you can use to forge this connection. Stories and examples allow you to transport your audience to new places, to offer them entertaining breaks from the serious content of your speech, and to add emotional content that stimulates memory and engages their senses. When you stir their feelings, they become more receptive to you and your message. Years after you've given a speech, people will tell you they once heard you speak, and didn't you tell the story about...? Your story rekindles the emotion you evoked in them and it guides them back to the points you made. Stories are powerful connectors.

Let's look at an example from a speech directed at young women living on their own while attending university or college. The objective was to have audience members take responsibility for their own personal safety. There were three main points in the speech: 1) how to identify your risks, 2) how to take steps to avoid risks, and 3) how to handle yourself when your safety is challenged. This story was used as the opening.

Angie, a co-worker of mine, is an avid distance runner. One night late last summer, she headed out for her usual run in the bushy country near her suburb. She described the evening as muggy and remembered how dense the air seemed. Every breath seemed to fill her lungs with the dust and smog of the day. Because clouds choked out the night sky and thick air obscured the lights from the city, it was too dark to see well on the dirt path surrounding her neighbourhood.

After a short time, she decided to abort her run and cut across some vacant land to her home. She heard her muffled footfalls and felt a little spurt of dust with each step. She heard her own ragged breathing. And every now and then she heard a sound she couldn't quite identify. The final few meters along the vacant lot took her beside a hedgerow. She felt the dusty leaves brush her arm when she ran too close to it and once a bare branch caught and momentarily tugged at her tee-shirt. She felt a tightening in her stomach and chest; a feeling she knew was panic. She sensed that she was not alone on the path.

There was something else, just on the other side of the hedge, or just behind her. She slowed to listen but heard nothing but the pounding of her own heart. She sped up and felt sure she heard something gasping for air. She called out, but got no answer. She stopped, turned suddenly, but neither saw nor heard anything. Full of fear and dread she raced along that narrow trail, colliding with the hedge and tangling in its branches, cursing her decision to run in such an isolated area, until finally she reached the back corner of her neighbour's lot. Safety and relief lay just ahead. She had only to turn slightly and squeeze through the wooden fence at the back of their lot. She paused, crouched slightly to make her move, and at that moment of safety within her reach, something reached from the hedge – and pulled her to the ground.

I usually leave the story at that point and await the reaction of my audience. I hear a collective gasp and see on their faces how involved they are in the story. I know these young women were there, in the scene, as I told it. I know they can empathize with Angie and can project her experience into their own lives. I know, at that moment, the power of connecting with my audience. When I tell them how to take responsibility for their personal safety, I know they are listening.

EDIT YOUR STORIES FOR MAXIMUM CONNECTION

A wise old speaker, Kenneth McFarland,[1] once said, *"It's a poor public speaker who can't tell a story better than it happened."* This means you have to examine your stories and select those aspects of each story that will best make your point and the connection with your audience. We collect stories all of our lives and then as speakers, we must edit and adapt those stories to help us connect with the listener. That means understanding the audience and identifying their beliefs.

My first efforts to use the *Angie story* weren't very successful. As I told it then, the distance runner, a young woman, had all the same feelings and sensations, but the setting was rural, and the climax of the story involved her nearly getting mowed down by a white-tailed deer. It was an event from my late teen years. Although I was able to win audience attention and entertain them, the conclusion didn't connect them to their own experiences and feelings. As one astute participant said, *"You don't really expect us to fear an attack by Bambi, do you?"* She got me thinking and I went back to work on the editing of my story.

While I was trying to improve the story, two things happened: a co-worker, Angie (hence the name of the story), was attacked by a human assailant while out running. He stepped out from behind a bush and pulled her to the ground; she fought him off and escaped. Angie's story triggered a memory of my own. My assailant was lingering near the entrance to the city park where I often ran. As I attempted to leave the park, he lunged at me. I screamed and raced away hearing his maniacal laughter behind me. The two stories from real life merged with the one I was working on to form a perfect story that connected the feelings, sensations, and experiences of my audience to the point I was making to them.

Whether you create stories based on your own experience, borrow from friends and acquaintances, or invent them, if you want your stories to connect your listener to you and your message, you must customize them. You need to consider the experiences of your audience and adjust your material to make it richly evocative and relevant to their lives.

CONNECT THROUGH YOUR CHARACTERS

Sometimes you can create a strong bond with your audience by choosing a central character they can admire or adore. Nearly everyone has a grandmother or a beloved older relative, which is part of the reason why this next example works.

The setting is usually a Toastmasters Club[2] and the objective is to improve recruitment. The speech has three points: 1) understand that people join an organization for their own reasons, 2) find out what their reasons are, and 3) encourage them to join by pitching to those reasons. This is a very basic sales speech for a general adult audience. The example is used to illustrate point one.

Grandmother Hope came from England as a young woman and had never lost her British dignity and style. She expected others to respect her and was quick to correct anyone who thought they could treat her otherwise. As her granddaughter, I was expected to visit regularly. I loved spending time with her but since I was often on a tight schedule, one time I decided to accomplish a couple of tasks at once. I invited her to accompany me to a Toastmasters Club near her home. Member ages ranged from early twenties to fifty-something, so Grandmother Hope stood out; she was already 89.

She enjoyed it greatly and on the way home she asked me, *"What are the qualifications to become a Toastmaster?"* I explained that you had to be eighteen years of age, pay the initiation and membership dues and, in this case be single since that was a requirement of the club we visited. Grandmother was quick to point out that she was old enough, could squeeze the dues from her meager pension (she could always squeeze something from her much maligned government income), and was indeed single. My grandfather had been dead for a couple of decades. Since Grandpa Bill, there had only been boyfriends and I think, at 89, she was tapering off on them too. So, Grandma qualified to join the Discovery Toastmasters Club, applied and became quite active.

Several years later I asked her, *"Grandmother, why do you like being a member of Toastmasters?"* I've never forgotten her answer because it so effectively makes my point about why people join an organization.

We expect people to join to learn speaking skills, gain confidence, practice listening, and develop leadership skills. We know many join for career enhancement and some join to improve their performance in their avocation, but her answer surprised me and reminded me how important it is to ask what potential members would like to get from their membership. She said, *"Well, dear, when you're my age everyone you know is dying. At Toastmasters, they aren't all about to die."*

This is a story that makes a point but also connects the group because of the feisty main figure, Grandmother Hope, who liked Toastmasters because she liked being around live people. As I tell the story, my listeners create their own mental image of the central character. They become involved in the mystery of why an octogenarian would want to join a business-oriented, personal enhancement organization. Best of all, they feel more comfortable with me because the story reveals a little of my personality and background. As one listener said, *"You seemed a little more human and vulnerable. I felt I could relate to you and understand your speech."*[3]

STORIES: POWERFUL CONNECTORS IN BUSINESS SPEECHES

So far you've seen stories used to illustrate speeches given to general audiences, but let's examine the use of stories in speeches where more formality would be appropriate, such as speaking to a potential investor.

The speaker has a database product to assist medical doctors and healthcare agencies to determine if and when patients have had certain treatments. The product prevents duplication of services, alerts health authorities to abuses of the system, and helps practitioners to determine if follow-up is required. The speaker is the genius behind the product, and he needs venture capital to fully develop his product and bring it to market.

He has an audience of one, a venture capitalist who has already looked at an initial proposal and decided the database product won't be successful because medical doctors won't want to pay for it. He is a semi-retired businessman with some background in healthcare, although as a Canadian he is most familiar with Canada's socialized healthcare system, and this product is for the American market where healthcare is more commercial in nature. The investor is said to have a poor attention span and at about seventy years old, is more focused on his family than on businesses requiring a lot of daily attention.

Because the data base product is already in use by several Health Management Organizations and a couple of small county health agencies, the speaker can use statistics and examples to support his presentation. He'll need to show that an acceptable return on investment is possible, that the product is sound, that the company is properly structured, and that he is the right person to lead the firm. All of these approaches are designed to appeal to an intellectual decision. A story will enhance the presentation by appealing to the emotional aspect of decision making. What follows is an approximation of the story used by the speaker. (This product isn't fully to market and so some information is obscured to protect the entrepreneur.)

Imagine your grandson, Harley, is on vacation in California with his parents – your son and his wife. Harley develops a problem with his breathing and is taken to a local hospital where a diagnosis of asthma is made and a drug is administered. After instruction regarding his care, his parents take Harley back to their hotel. The doctors have said it was a very mild attack and unlikely to cause further problems, so believing the problem is under control, the family continues their holiday as planned.

Two days later, in another county, Harley has a more severe attack and struggles for breath and life. This time, he is staying with close family friends while his parents are away for a couple of days on their own. The friends never thought to find out what treatments were given. Perhaps Harley's parents didn't even know themselves, and certainly little Harley can't tell anyone. But, fortunately, a quick check of the database tells the new physician what drug was administered and allows her to quickly determine an appropriate treatment. Your grandson, Harley, is alive and healthy because of a database that allows the medical system to communicate essential information when family, friends, the patient, and previous medical experts cannot.

This is an example of a *for instance* story. It is based on a real problem in healthcare, but the resolution of the problem and the story itself are fictional. The main characters are created just for this listener. The speaker knew this investor's priority was his family and in conversation, just before he presented, he learned the investor's oldest grandson was named Harley, so he was able to make the story quite realistic for the investor. The teller and the listener knew this story was created just for the purpose of the presentation, but its telling made all the difference. The investor listened and has made an initial commitment to provide venture capital.

LIMIT THE DETAIL, EVOKE EMOTIONS

The story just related had the desired effect even though the example was essentially fictional and the circumstances seemed a bit unlikely. Why did it connect? It was personalized to the audience which certainly helped. It was simple and specific with just enough detail to make the point, and thus well-matched to someone who isn't a patient listener. But, it had another noteworthy strength.

Harley's story allowed the speaker to show how his product would make a real difference in the lives of others. His potential investor is reaching a stage in his life where he wants to give back to his family and his community. While other information about the product might appeal to his rational mind, the detail in this story appealed to his emotions. He found himself liking the entrepreneur more, therefore wanting to support his business if the plans and projections otherwise met his criteria.

From the examples you've just read, you can see that stories can be told exactly as they happened, they can be the amalgamation of several experiences, or they can even be somewhat fictional. In each example, you can see the need to carefully select and limit the detail you use in creating your stories. You can also see the incredible power of connecting to the emotions of the listener.

You might have noticed in the story about Angie, my co-worker, I don't tell you how old she is, what job she does, whether or not she is married, and I don't even tell you much about her interest in running. These details are unimportant and would only obscure the story. Choose details that are evocative and appropriate to the point you are making. *"She heard her muffled footfalls and felt a little spurt of dust with each step."*, summons a rich image for the listener while telling you she works with computers creates little or no helpful imagery.

LIMIT THE LENGTH OR USE SUBCLIMAXES

Just as it is important to carefully select details with your audience and goal in mind, it is important to limit the length of your story. If you can tell your story within a couple of minutes, it will quickly support your point. If your story is much longer you risk the audience forgetting what point you were making. You also risk losing their attention unless it is a compelling story. Compelling stories have a logical build and a great climax or resolution.

You can use longer stories, but you'll need to have one or more subclimaxes to help hold attention and add interim reminders to keep the audience focused on the point of your story. This next example is quite long but it illustrates the use of sub-climaxes and interim reminders.

I use this story in my seminars on networking to help my audiences become aware of their need for building and maintaining a support system. Before launching into the story, I have given my listeners several reasons why it is important to have a network for business purposes, but I am now introducing the idea of a network as essential for personal support.

Returning home from an extended trip with my husband, I phoned my parents who had also just returned from vacation. They had travelled by bus with a group of senior citizens from their home in central British Columbia, through the magnificent canyons of Utah and Arizona. Their trip was to have concluded with a visit to the north rim of the Grand Canyon. They had looked forward for many years to this excursion, and I was excited to hear all about it. I called very early in the morning when they would normally be home and was surprised when several calls went unanswered.

Worried that something had gone wrong, I called my older brother, Ted, who quickly provided me with some sketchy details. My fears were confirmed; something had happened.

As the bus tour headed southwards, my father had become more and more ill. His breathing problems had become so serious that he was evacuated by helicopter from the north rim of the Grand Canyon to the intensive care unit in the small city of Flagstaff, Arizona. Ted said Dad was doing well but perhaps I should contact Mom who was having to cope on her own with the medical decisions.

I remember the stress in her voice; she was coping, but it was taking a toll. It didn't take long to find out her two main concerns; one was amusing and the other completes this story.

Worry number one was money. In Canada we hear such tales of the astronomical cost of American medical care, and we know our Canadian medical insurance doesn't begin to cover the costs of treatments outside our own system. Therefore, when we travel outside Canada, most of us buy special policies. My parents were always prudent in this matter and had extensive medical insurance. But my mother, feeling the stress of having a critically ill mate, was sure they wouldn't be allowed out of Arizona without paying the entire medical bill in cash. I assured her that American hospitals would accept her credit card, and if there was a problem we'd all chip in to bail them out. Despite her stress Mom managed to see the humour in how she had interpreted her financial circumstances. (This provides a subclimax and an opportunity for the audience to relax for a moment.)

Her second concern regarded transporting my father back to British Columbia. Although he was still in intensive care, the doctors felt he could travel back to Canada as long as he had oxygen. I didn't think this would be a problem because on most commercial airplanes, during the safety briefing, they tell us oxygen, if needed, will flow from the overhead compartment. So I phoned a major Canadian airline and was told it would take one week to get permission to use what they called, "cabin oxygen."

Think about that. Now I don't know about you, but I certainly hope it doesn't take that long to get approval if we are up there flying and something happens to the air supply. I couldn't believe the airline's response. (This provides a second subclimax and usually an opportunity for some laughter.)

I thought it was silly to leave my father in hospital for a week, so I phoned the competing airline thinking surely they would handle the problem better. They gave me a similar story. They were sure that within seven to ten working days they could get approval for the use of cabin oxygen and have Dad flown from Flagstaff to Phoenix, then Phoenix to Los Angeles, then Los Angeles to Seattle, then Seattle to Vancouver, and finally Vancouver to Kelowna, the nearest airport to their home. They told me they could complete this plane journey in a mere three days. (Incidentally, this is also how long it takes to drive the distance in a car.) Imagine a seventy year old, just released from intensive care, expected to travel for three days, getting on and off planes, in and out of hotels, and always with the need for portable oxygen. I was furious and also extremely frustrated. I am used to making things happen.

In frustration, over the next few hours my husband and I told many of our friends and acquaintances about the problems we were having with the airlines. We were using our networks for support. All were sympathetic and several had useful suggestions, but we were astounded when one friend offered us the use of his private jet.

I don't know about you, but I didn't know we had any friends who owned private jets. Do any of you have a friend with a private jet parked out back? (This represents a third subclimax and an opportunity to interact with the audience.) Well we discovered one, and he offered to help us retrieve my father as soon as the jet was available. As it turned out, the next day was the one day the jet was not booked for corporate work, and by coincidence it was also the one day in the next eight days that I wasn't booked somewhere to speak or teach. If I could be at the Executive Airport in Vancouver by 6 a.m., we could bring Dad home the next day. The doctors in Flagstaff approved of the idea and we were set.

The next morning we left at dawn flying into Boise, Idaho, where we had to set down to clear U.S. Customs and Immigration. As I climbed from the small jet, I was astonished to find two gentlemen rolling red carpet out to our airplane. I was further amazed when the staff at the Executive Airport handed me a cup of coffee and directed me to a telephone so I could contact Flagstaff hospital and let them know when we would be arriving. After a quick discussion with the officials at the airport, we were back onto our plane bound for Arizona. I was surprised at the speed of our departure until the co-pilot explained our med-evac status. All other air traffic had been held while we came and went from the airport.

Perhaps you were raised like I was and don't like a fuss being made over you if no fuss is required. Med-evac status sounded like a lot of fuss to me. Earlier in the day I'd packed several days supplies in case my dad wasn't well enough to travel all the way home, but now I began to worry that he might not seem ill at all and we'd all be embarrassed. Our arrival in Flagstaff seemed much like our arrival in Boise, Idaho. There was the red carpet, the coffee, and the use of telephones, and once again, to facilitate our med-evac all other planes had been diverted or delayed. As my parents arrived at the airport my tension mounted.

I needn't have worried, for although he looked nicely rested my father was towing a small tank of oxygen and was connected to it by some sort of clear plastic tubing. Little prongs directed the oxygen-enriched air into his nostrils. I was grateful for that life-saving air supply, not only because it meant we could get him home, but also because it clearly defined his illness as serious.

We all enjoyed that flight home as we had enough time to hear of each other's adventures and view a most beautiful section of the United States. In slightly less than three hours, thanks to a generous tailwind, we landed at the Kelowna airport. Geography isn't important, but you need to understand that few private jets fly directly from the U.S. into this small city so we were a welcome diversion for the Customs and Immigration officer.

Our pilot asked us to stay in our seats because he felt we lacked sufficient paperwork to import the oxygen equipment, and he wanted to speak with the Canadian Customs and Immigration official outside the aircraft. But before the pilot could reach the immigration officer, he had stormed up the steps into the small plane. I knew our pilot was worried because government officials have as much power as they want to detain a plane in such a situation, and he wanted to return to his home base in Vancouver.

None of us could afford to be delayed but here was this burly immigration officer in the plane looking directly at the offending oxygen equipment. My heart sank. It had all gone so well to this point; my networking had done its job, but there didn't seem much I could do to smooth relations with the massive, unsmiling officer.

This man then looked directly at my father and immediately bellowed, *"David Hope! What the heck are you doing here?"* It seems the immigration officer was an acquaintance of my father's as they were members of the same fraternal organization. Soon we were all shaking hands, laughing and relaxing. If there were any formalities at Customs and Immigration, I have no memory of them. I do remember the Customs agent helping us transport my parents, their luggage, and the oxygen tank through the airport to a waiting car.

My husband's network helped us arrange the mercy flight, and my father's network smoothed our way through Customs and Immigration. But, if you're following the story closely, you might be wondering, just where a waiting car came from? That was through a third network. My brother, realizing he could not reach Kelowna in time to meet our plane, called his in-laws who lived nearby and arranged for them to meet us at the airport and take care of my parents until he could arrive.

This story has a happy ending because my father enjoyed many years of health thanks to the medical investigation of his condition that was done in Arizona. I love to tell this story and recall all the fears and joys of that time, but for me it is really about the need we all have for connections with others. It is about how people reach out to others, and how we need to be willing to help when we can and accept help when we need it.

You'll likely agree that this story is long, but I know it connects with my listeners. As I tell it I get a lot of reaction, and after my seminars it is the story listeners most often refer to. Months after I've given the speech someone in the audience will meet me somewhere else and say, *"I remember you. You told us the story about rescuing your father in a private jet."* As a speaker you know it's a compliment if your audience remembers anything you said, but it's an amazing compliment if they can tell you why you said it. So I test for meaning and ask listeners, *"Do you remember why I told that story?"* Answers vary, but most tell me it convinced them or reminded them of how much we need to rely on each other and how powerful a network is in providing that support. Bingo! It's a long story, but it wins attention, connects with the audience, and makes the point.

As you read the story you probably noticed the two features I mentioned in introducing it. I used several interim references to the support networking provides because that was the whole point of the story. I also interrupted the story a couple of times to interact with the audience and let them enjoy some of the humour of the whole situation. If you choose lengthy stories to illustrate your points, you will need to find ways like this to keep the audience attentive and focused on your goals.

Stories let us add colour and life to the points we need to make and that helps the listener stay attentive. Stories tap into the emotions of our listeners helping them to make decisions emotionally as well as intellectually. Stories help our listeners recall our presentations. Best of all, stories help our listeners feel comfortable with us. Stories connect us to our audience.

SUMMARY: USE STORIES TO CONNECT

- Invent, edit, or arrange each story for your audience and objective.
- Evoke emotion – we remember better if the story touches us.
- Choose worthy or memorable characters.
- Limit detail.
- Be brief – try to tell your stories in less than two minutes.
- Use subclimaxes to hold attention in longer stories.

Notes

[1] Kenneth McFarland, Golden Gavel Address, Toastmasters International Convention, Milwaukee, WI, 1980.

[2] Toastmasters International is a world-wide organization helping members improve their communication and leadership skills. It is a non-profit educational organization working with members in 8400 clubs, operating in 68 countries.

For more information contact: tminfo@toastmasters.org

[3] After each Toastmaster speech, the speaker receives written and oral evaluation. It isn't possible to credit this comment to a particular individual because written evaluations are anonymous.

CHAPTER 6

USE BAD MOMENTS TO CONNECT

SOMEONE IN THE AUDIENCE DISAGREES OPENLY WITH YOU, YOU CAN'T quite recall the correct name for something but you know every expert in your audience will, your sound system explodes just as you begin a major speech, or you respond to an audience question and then can't recall where you were in your speech. These are but a few of the bad moments speakers tell about. And it is in these bad moments where we often get our best opportunities to connect with an audience and win both their attention and their willingness to do what we ask.

I learned this lesson when I fell through a stage while delivering a major address on the topic of body language. My audience were all travel agents; we'd all travelled to Barbados for their annual meeting and they'd begun the evening before with a wild party. I was scheduled to keynote the first afternoon. The morning speaker, Jeff, talked for four hours although he was scheduled to speak for only three. He'd given them a break about ten a.m., but otherwise his audience were in their seats for the entire time. And they were cold. The audience shivered in shorts and tee-shirts because someone had maximized the air conditioning. Jeff finished just after twelve noon, but two suppliers who had sponsored the morning had been promised an opportunity to speak too. So, although it was lunchtime, and although everyone could smell the food awaiting them outside the meeting room, ninety very cold travel agents huddled politely through another half-hour of speeches.

Finally they got lunch and a welcome chance to warm up in the sun but were told to be in my session thirty minutes later because we were now behind schedule. They weren't in a pleasant mood.

Furthermore, someone had complained of being cold, so during lunch the air conditioning was turned off and now the room was hot and humid. I began my speech with an audience that was hot, tired, stuffed with food they'd consumed too rapidly, and simply uncooperative. I felt sure of my opening, yet it didn't move them a bit. I knew I was dying up there in front of a critical audience, but I swear I didn't wish for the earth to open and swallow me up.

About fifteen minutes into the speech, still with very poor audience response and no sense of connecting with them, I fell through the stage. Not entirely through the stage and out of sight. That would have been preferable. No, I just put the heel of my shoe through what I'd thought was a solid piece of wood. Burlap had been used to cover two risers comprising the stage, and right there in the middle of the stage was a hidden cleft and I hit it. I knew I was now connected to the stage if not my audience. They had no idea what was going on.

I was wearing high heels and a bright yellow suit, telling my audience how they could use movement to enhance their presentations, and here I was, effectively nailed to the stage. I scrunched my toes in my shoe in an effort to leverage the heel from the stage, but it didn't budge. I tried lifting my heel from the shoe and dragging my foot forward, but the burlap prevented lateral movement along the cleft. Nothing worked.

I knew I should try to make a joke about the situation, but your mind plays terrible tricks on you when you're faced with a crisis. The only joke that came to my mind was the Mommy-Mommy type. You might remember these jokes from your own childhood. They were gross tales told by pre-adolescents in an effort to disgust adults. I could hardly use that sort of material with a business audience, could I?

In desperation I excused myself, removed my shoe, bent over, and wrenched my pump from the cleft in the stage, and for the first time got a visibly positive response from my audience. I had no idea they'd enjoy my predicament, but clearly they did. I told them what had happened and they practically howled. I was standing on stage in only one high heel and moving as if I had a major limp, and they were loving it.

My instinct told me they'd laugh at anything about now, so I told them that pre-adolescent joke, *"Mommy-Mommy, I'm tired of going in circles. Shut-up dear, or I'll nail your other foot to the floor."* They roared. Since the speech was already interrupted, I asked if someone could turn on a small amount of air conditioning so I wouldn't have to remove my clothes as well as my shoes. That too got an appreciative cheer. After that their response to my speech was positive and at times greatly exceeded my expectations.

My worst moment had given me the opportunity to connect with a very difficult audience. As I worked with them in smaller groups over the next few days and enjoyed them, I realized how fortunate the shoe incident was. It had connected us in the way any disaster unites the survivors.

As a speaker you will have some bad moments; in fact, the more you speak, the more you'll have. These bad moments will also become some of your most treasured speaking memories as you turn your calamities into connections. In addition to the stage incident I mentioned, I've forgotten a key word at a critical moment, had an overhead projector catch on fire as I spoke, and discovered a naked child parading behind me as I presented. Perhaps the most distressing disasters are when someone in your audience says or implies they don't respect you. In all these situations, asking your audience for help is the best way to deal with the crisis.

CONNECT BY ASKING THEM FOR HELP

When you forget the term or word for something, simply ask the audience for help. I've done this countless times and am amazed by how helpful an audience can be. The experts in the audience get a chance to display their talents, I get a chance to interact with them, and I prove conclusively that I'm as fallible as they are. I've asked audiences afterwards if they minded helping me with my speech, and they universally claim to not mind at all. So, if your worst disaster or worst fear is forgetfulness, let it go. Simply involve your audience in the remedy.

I was speaking at a law firm when the overhead projector began to sizzle and smoke. I always take along my own projector, but they insisted I use theirs as it was brand new and they wanted to see it used effectively. I was delighted to experiment with it because, while most overhead projectors are simple, this one had many exciting technical features.

As you probably know, many new electronic devices emit some smell when they are first being used, but this projector really was making a stench. Finally I commented on it to my audience, who had seemed a little distracted during the opening of my session. They admitted they too were concerned about the blue smoke seeping from their side of the overhead. I hit the power switch just as the first bright flame escaped from the machine. Seconds later we had it unplugged and, with much laughter and joking, retired the sizzling projector onto an adjoining concrete patio, replacing it with my trusty old low-tech portable overhead. Again, we were united by our near disaster, and when I forgot a participant's name during the session, I blamed it on smoke inhalation. Months later when I returned to the law firm a new group of seminar participants asked if I'd be performing my famous pyrotechnics.

The naked child is a far less likely disaster but certainly shows that the more speaking you do, the more opportunities you'll have for truly weird problems. I was speaking at a convention in Florida when I suddenly became aware that my audience wasn't paying attention to me. Their eyes were all focused forward as if they were seeing me, but I got the strange feeling I'd become invisible. Then there were the muffled giggles, nudging, and whispers. Finally I paused and glanced behind me; then I turned from my audience and stared. The drapes at the back of the stage, closed in every other session I'd attended, had been pulled open. Revealed was a glass partition which separated the ballroom from the narrow walkway to the pool. I don't know how many people had walked behind me as I spoke, but the cause of the laughter and whispering was a delightful little girl, perhaps two or three years old, stark naked except for her bathing suit dangling from one hand. She was obviously waiting, none too patiently, for her mother, who, seeing an entire auditorium enjoying her daughter's performance, raised her hands shoulder high in the universal signal for, *"I give up!"* and marched the child off her impromptu stage. An equally embarrassed hotel employee drew the drapes, and I had my audience back.

This incident presented a dilemma. I could ignore the problem and return to my planned speech, or I could enjoy the moment with my audience and the connection that child had created for us. I was caught between the two, not quite sure how to proceed. Then a fellow in the front row gave me my line, *"If you'd known nudity would be so successful with this audience, I bet you'd have tried it yourself."* He said it really loudly, got a great laugh, and all I had to do was pretend to take off my jacket and then thank him. Another disaster was diverted thanks to the quick response by a clever participant, after which the audience quickly warmed to my presentation.

These examples have become useful stories and fond memories

for me. I recall less fondly those few times when someone has declared or indicated, in front of my entire audience, a lack of respect for me or my material. These unpleasant situations can still provide an opportunity to connect with your audience. A couple of examples will help you if you ever face a similar situation.

EVEN A HECKLER CAN HELP YOU CONNECT

I was speaking to about twenty members of the Dental Surgeons Speaker's Bureau. I'd worked with most of them before, and I already felt a comfortable rapport with them. I opened my session with a couple of anecdotes about outrunning bears. I'm sure everyone knew they were fictional, but they seemed to enjoy them. Then I asked each participant to introduce himself (they were all male) and tell us what topic he most frequently addressed as part of the speaker's bureau. The first speaker told us he was an endodontist and chiefly spoke about the role of diet in dental health, the next had a pediatric dental practice and liked to speak to expectant and new mothers about their opportunities to influence their children's dental health, and so it went.

About six speakers into the exercise, a gentleman I hadn't met before introduced himself, paused, and said, *"I don't find either of your opening stories appropriate."* He sat down to thunderous silence. The audience awaited my response. I felt brain dead. I knew this was a critical moment in the seminar, but I hadn't a clue how to handle the situation. This was quite early in my speaking career, and I was certain it would be my last professional speech. Then I heard myself thank the speaker for his opinion and call on the next participant. The seminar went on with the other participants rising to the occasion, each saying something more amusing than the last. They were rallying to support me.

There is a saying I remember from first aid training that, roughly goes, *"...at least do no harm."* It's a good rule for speakers faced with an awkward moment because there is potential to do harm. If I'd invited discussion with this prickly personality, I'd likely have heard more damaging information. Had he become more outspoken, I might have slipped to his level of behaviour and would certainly have felt worse about myself. If I'd argued with him or ridiculed his lack of social skills, there is a chance the audience would have rallied behind him. The secret to connecting when one person attacks is to keep the rest of the audience on your side.

Following that seminar, no less than six of the twenty participants came to me separately to tell me how much they appreciated
my response. Apparently this dentist was well known for his outspoken comments, and some of them had felt the sting of his comments
during previous association meetings and other speaker's bureau
events. As further proof that my problem was successfully handled,
the group invited me back to speak and asked me to give advice on
how to handle difficult audience members.

STAY CALM TO CONNECT

Another memorable challenge occurred when I was teaching a two-
day presentation skills course for administrative staff at a university. I
had phoned each participant before the course, so I knew that half of
the participants were working primarily as teaching assistants (T.A.'s)
and were volunteer facilitators for an on-campus program designed to
assist new T.A.'s in the art of instructional facilitation. Most participants wanted to be better presenters, but two were self-described
experts looking to see if someone from outside the university (me)
had anything new to offer. Although skilled and experienced, they also
both assured me they wanted to learn from my session and would
contribute their own expertise in any way they could.

The first day of the course was enjoyable. My two experts,
although very good friends, sat across the room from each other and
made positive contributions. Early on during the second day, each
participant was asked to make a short presentation as part of a session
on vocal improvement. They were to express strong emotion, so I
recommended they tell us about something that made them annoyed,
frustrated, angry, or perhaps even joyful. One of my experts volun-
teered to go first. She rose, looked at me, and using exceptional vocal
variety said, *"I hate it when people assume I'm heterosexual."* As with the
dentist I mentioned in my last example, this brief comment was a
show-stopper. There was dead silence and I knew I was being tested.

What went through my mind was all sorts of self-recriminations.
What had I done to create this situation? Was I guilty as charged? Was
she really talking about me or had something else happened in the
room, something I wasn't aware of? I'm not inclined to pay attention
to a participant's sexual preference, but being heterosexual I could certainly have unwittingly made some comment that made her uncomfortable. And, on this particular university campus, there was certainly
a group of women who wanted the rest of us sensitized to the topic.

Guilt was decidedly fogging my brain, and so I was once again surprised to hear myself say, *"Excellent vocal variety. Next —"* and see myself indicating the next participant. I have no idea what the next few participants said, but somehow we got through that tough moment. At the next break I was approached by two participants who apologized for their co-worker's behaviour and thanked me for the way I handled it. I never did feel a strong connection with the T.A. who challenged me, but the rest of the group rallied to my support and gave me strong reviews afterwards. [1]

This incident reminded me of a couple of key points: no matter how long you have been a speaker or presenter, you will still face challenges, and those challenges will give you an opportunity to connect or bond with your audience. There isn't a right answer or correct response to this kind of situation, but you owe it to your audience to behave with dignity and take the leadership role. If you lead, they will follow and follow gratefully because you've provided a simple effective pathway for them.

Turning lemons into lemonade to connect

I've given you some examples from my own experience, but I've also seen how other speakers have broken through the barriers with an audience and truly connected when something went wrong. With close to a thousand in his audience, a keynote speaker was interrupted when his sound system exploded. The hotel crew worked as rapidly as possible to replace the unit, but the speaker was left for nearly twenty minutes without amplification. With nothing but body language to work with, he gave the performance of a lifetime. He demonstrated, he had us demonstrate, he got people at the front to run to the back relaying his message, he had us laughing, clapping, and cheering. He finished his ninety-minute session to a standing ovation and the admiration of that enormous audience. He could have been forgiven for abandoning the speech, but he chose instead to turn the problem into an opportunity. [2]

Provide leadership

I've heard speakers worry that they might die as they give a speech, but another professional speaker tells of actually having a man die during his speech. This speaker took control, had someone call 911, and united the audience in silent prayer while the elderly gentleman received first aid and was removed from the room. Although the group wasn't there because of religious affiliation, after the man was taken from the room they continued to pray together. Someone who knew the man then said a few words about him and assured the group that his friend would want them to continue their program. True, the atmosphere was subdued, but a bond developed in that group because they'd weathered this event together. When bad things happen, they tend to forge a natural connection, and as speakers, we have only to provide appropriate leadership.

Sometimes something bad happens beyond the scope of the assembly, but it affects your audience and so it affects you as a speaker. I was in Palm Springs, California, when Congressman Sonny Bono died[3] in a ski accident. At a luncheon meeting the next day, there was a pall over the group. Several speakers mentioned the death but did nothing to raise our spirits. Then Paul Sickler[4] spoke up and said he felt particularly badly about Bono's death because he had published an article the previous week in which he criticized an aspect of Bono's congressional record. He said he'd known Sonny for many years and admired him greatly, so he regretted the critical piece he'd last written. Paul then went on to say that this situation reminded him of how we never know how long we have with anyone and how important it is to let others know they are respected, loved, and appreciated. Paul did two things for me in the way he spoke about the tragedy: he lifted my spirits by giving the event some useful meaning, and he made me want to walk over and introduce myself. He connected where other speakers did not because he showed leadership in handling the events of the day.

EMPATHIZE TO CONNECT

Another problem turned into an opportunity for me when I was to address an early morning program for the cashiers of a retail chain. These were all fairly young women from small towns and cities, many from rural areas. They were unsophisticated and somewhat shy, yet excited about the opportunity to spend time in a large city. Each cashier there had been chosen by her peers to represent them at this program, and they considered it both an honour and a responsibility to attend every event. I'd spoken at this program before and knew how seriously they regarded it.

I arrived a little later than I'd have liked and took a few minutes to check out the room where I'd be speaking before joining the group for breakfast. By the time I got to the breakfast, they were all standing around their tables, many with their heads bowed or eyes cast down as a distinguished looking older gentleman spoke at the microphone. I didn't immediately hear what he was saying, but as the president of this retail chain is known to have a strong Christian affiliation, I assumed he was offering a blessing.

But the blessing went on and on, and although I stayed just outside the meeting room, I noticed one of the few men in the room beckoning me to join them at his table. I wouldn't normally walk into a room during an invocation, so I hesitated and gave my attention to the speaker. His head reverently bowed over his notes, I heard him say, "...and for your lighter days, ladies, we have...." It took me a few seconds to realize the speaker represented a supplier of what is delicately referred to as feminine hygiene products. The sign behind his head proclaimed his company as the breakfast sponsor, and he had not-so-delicately chosen this opportunity to advertise its products to these captive young women.

By the time I crossed the room, I'd become aware of the embarrassed expressions on the women's faces and the equally uncomfortable expressions on the faces of the male managers serving as hosts at each table. These were not people accustomed to discussing feminine hygiene concerns publicly over coffee and eggs. Suppressed giggles, chortles of laughter, and finally generalized mirth broke out before the speaker had the good sense to stop talking. The folks at my table then told me the rest of the story. Mr. Hygiene, as they had now nicknamed him, had apparently arrived with a huge box full of samples, and as each woman arrived he had attempted to provide a sample. Many had declined his offer, so he'd also circulated throughout the room and offered the samples again once the women were seated. Laughter was the only appropriate response.

I left the breakfast before my audience did in order to make a final check of my room, so I missed the next chapter in their misery. With samples still remaining, he tried to give delegates another package as they left the breakfast room, and then moved his box to the door of my room for one last attempt. By the time they got to my meeting space, they hardly knew which way to look. Some were enjoying the humour, but a great many were embarrassed and humiliated. They were in no mood for my speech, and I knew I had to do something to help them get past the breakfast assault.

Humour, the topic of my next chapter, is definitely a powerful tool in such situations, but as I began speaking, I couldn't think of anything amusing to say without being rude to Mr. Hygiene, who was, after all, just doing his job. I opened to a reserved reception and quite rapidly moved into a preview of my keynote and a section I call housekeeping items. I told them when their next break would occur, invited questions anytime, explained the use of the notebook, and then said, *"...and in my session, I think you will be relieved to know, there will be no free samples."* A standing ovation is a great compliment from any audience, but when they rose from their seats cheering and clapping, I knew I'd connected and in so doing had provided the leadership necessary to get us past something negative that had happened beyond the scope of my presentation.

Summary: Use bad moments to connect

- Welcome the gifts of the moment – they're often more valuable than anything you could have planned.
- Let your audience help you – they'll love the opportunity to contribute.
- Humour is powerful – laugh at yourself, or at the moment if you can.
- Don't pick on anyone – it's the quickest way to lose audience support.
- Don't criticize or condemn anyone else's behaviour.
- Provide leadership – lead your audience to higher ground.

Notes

[1] A week later, still licking my wounds, I described the event over lunch with one of the professors from the university. She'd heard my course was very successful but hadn't heard about the T.A. As soon as I told the story, she identified the T.A. by name and told me she was practically famous on campus for such behaviour. I no longer felt special, and for once in my life, that was fine!

[2] James 'Doc' Blakely, Keynote Address, Toastmasters International Convention, Palm Desert, CA, 1989.

[3] 1935-1998. According to the January 6, 1998 edition of The Desert Sun newspaper, Bono died January 5 in a ski accident at Heavenly Ski Resort. Sonny Bono was serving his second term in the US Congress,

was mayor of Palm Springs from 1988 to 1992, and was more widely known for his earlier career as a singer and entertainer with his second wife, Cher.

[4] Paul Sickler, Toastmasters of the Desert, Palm Springs, CA, 1998.

CHAPTER 7

USE HUMOUR TO CONNECT

FROM THE PREVIOUS CHAPTER YOU HAVE SEEN THE VALUE OF PROVOKING laughter in your audience. Causing laughter isn't essential in speaking, but it is a powerful connector. Like stories, humour tends to help the audience feel we are human and a lot like them, so it breaks the artificial barrier between speaker and audience. Humour also helps speakers connect because, like stories, it holds the audience's attention, it helps clarify the points being made, and it makes those points memorable. It also lets us laugh, move, take in a deep breath or, as humorist Dr. Charlie Jarvis[1] often said, *"When they laugh they get a chance to adjust their underwear and that just makes them feel so much better."* Laughter is an effective icebreaker and serves equally well as a way to break tension or give the group a needed respite periodically in a detailed and serious speech.

EVERYONE CAN FIND WAYS TO USE HUMOUR

Although few speakers have told me they thought humour was a poor idea in speaking, many have told me they thought they lacked talent or had been born without some essential funny bone. Others, most often business and technical speakers, claimed they avoided it in their present type of speaking. Nevertheless, I've met only a few speakers who couldn't move an audience to mirth once they worked at it. I believe almost everyone can use humour effectively, but most of us do have to work at it. I've also seen humour used with excellent results in a wide variety of settings, so I wouldn't advise any speaker to declare humour off-bounds for certain types of speeches.

Perhaps the most common reason speakers avoid humour is

their quite natural fear of disasters. An audience laughing at an appropriate time gives you a lot of confidence to continue speaking and take additional risks. But, what if the opposite happens, and no one responds to your amusing anecdote or witty turn of phrase, what if you bomb? I can't promise you a bomb-free presentation under any circumstances, but I can suggest some ways to use humour to connect with your audience that are unlikely to cause a disaster.

HUMOUR CONNECTS WHEN IT SURPRISES THE AUDIENCE

Humour tends to work because it surprises the audience. It is more likely to be funny to them if they can relate to the topic but wouldn't be embarrassed by it. For this reason, you'll find it easiest to spawn merriment if you know your audience very well. When I attend or speak at service clubs, I am always impressed by the amount of laughter certain remarks can generate, even though as an outsider I don't have a prayer of understanding why they are funny. These "inside" jokes have helped me to understand the nature of humour and also to learn to craft my own material.

START WITH THE FUNNIEST THING IN THE ROOM – YOU

The safest place to begin in crafting your own humour is with yourself. A good friend of mine, Dougie,[2] is about five and a half feet tall, or as he says, *"vertically challenged."* He has poked fun at his own diminutive stature for as long as I've known him, and when asked to stand to speak frequently begins his talk by saying, *"I'm Doug Anderson and I am standing."* He is much loved for his ability to laugh at himself.

I'm not Doug Anderson and my stature isn't remarkable in any way so I can't trade on that. I am, however, noted for speaking rather quickly, something you won't be able to tell if you are simply reading my book. I've learned this is a great place to start my presentations because it saves some people in my audience from worrying that I don't know I speak quickly and from having to come up after my speech to point this out to me. So I just warn them right up front and tell them it's actually a benefit to them.

First I say, *"I want to warn you right up front, I talk quickly. Have any of you noticed that?"* There are always a few who raise their hands or visibly let me know they've noticed. I then tell the rest of the group the reason they don't think I talk fast is because they talk quickly too. They seem to like that as I'm sure plenty of them have been told to slow down, themselves.

Next I tell them my fast pace is actually an advantage to them and discuss a study showing we listen three to five times faster than anyone speaks. I then mention research that shows how they'll use the additional time if I speak too slowly. *"Apparently, some of you will worry about the work you've left behind in your workplace, some of you will worry about your social lives (those of you who actually have one), and some will have fantasies – as I speak."* This generally produces some chuckles and at least one person (frequently male) will usually blush a nice pink colour and laugh deeply. If I know the blusher, I might ask if him there's anything the rest of us should know, but if I don't know him I just gaze in his direction and look slightly surprised. This frivolity lets the audience know I don't take myself too seriously after which they easily respond to additional teasing. The initial connection has been made.

Although I play with the audience to some extent during this opener, I primarily rely on self-deprecating humour. I believe audiences enjoy this type of humour if you use it infrequently, but if it is overused, they feel you are putting yourself down. One speaker I know frequently mentions that others avoid her because of her prickly personality. When she first mentions her somewhat abrasive style, almost everyone laughs, but when she refers to it repeatedly, her listeners start to display signs of discomfort.

Although there isn't a rule, I'd recommend limiting yourself to two or three self-deprecating remarks in any speech; make them believable, but as innocuous as possible. You're unlikely to get a positive audience response from comments about the wrinkled condition of your attire, how long you've kept your audience waiting, your flatulence, or infertility. Stand-up comedians might create routines around these topics and have their audience rolling in the aisles, but for most of us, good taste must prevail.

You need to be very comfortable with the label you use for yourself. Being vertically challenged, follicly challenged (bald), a motor mouth or even rotund might work for you, if you feel comfortable about it. If you have strong sensitivity to or negative feelings about the image you use in your self-deprecating humour, avoid it. One superb speaker I know gave an excellent speech about being temporarily confined to a wheelchair. I remember her mimicking those who treated her like some sort of imbecile or child saying, *"Would we like to use the bathroom before we go for a plane ride?"* This same speaker has an artificial limb, but as far as I know, never refers to it in jest. I think she is wise to avoid a topic that could make her or her audience feel uncomfortable.

Most humour aimed at yourself will help the audience relate to you but you have to consider the situation. John Nichols,[3] while delivering a slide show worried aloud, *"I have a terrible feeling this next slide is out of order but I'll just keep speaking as if it's not.",* and a couple of slides later he got another laugh with, *"Here's another slide out of order but I'll coolly take this in my stride."* If John hadn't been delivering a fine speech with excellent visual support, or if his audience had been tense and businesslike, these comments could have annoyed them. But John did know his audience. They were on their vacations at a hobby convention; there wasn't a business suit in the room, and he'd spent his time walking about and talking to various delegates as they arrived to hear his speech. It was a well-calculated risk.

TAKE SAFE AIM AT INANIMATE OBJECTS

Lampooning yourself is reasonably safe, but it certainly isn't the only option. Humour aimed at inanimate objects is also usually safe. John Nichols,[4] speaking about shortline railroads in Great Britain, first identified his expertise by saying he'd spent his last twelve summer vacations seeking out these fast disappearing railroads. As proof he had suffered enough to deliver such a speech with authority, he mentioned that British invention, the toast rack, and noted it as, *"hot toast anathema."* The toast rack was an amusing way to emphasize his abundant experience in Britain and hardly risky given that few North Americans prefer air-cooled dry toast.

A good friend and fine speaker, Judy Johnson,[5] has a terrific speech where she addresses the challenges of donning pantyhose. Although few men have personal experience with the topic, they seem to be as amused as the women who more commonly struggle with this modern invention. By contrast, an artist giving lessons on a cruise ship (how to paint a landscape in an hour) repeatedly tried to get a laugh from comments about her girdle. The audience were mostly under forty years old and they didn't find it amusing. I think an older cruising audience might have found it hilarious, but our art teacher didn't appreciate the difference age can make to whether or not humour will work.

Nowhere am I more aware of this than in my work with Rotary Youth Leadership Award (RYLA) delegates[6] who are a youthful eighteen to twenty-five. At the lower end of the age group, they haven't even graduated from high school while at the upper end some work, some attend college, and some are married or even raising a family. They will laugh when I speak about my pace of delivery and their potential fantasies. They are less likely to laugh at humour regarding my work with a law firm or my teaching public speaking to accountants and engineers. Such stories depend on the stereotyping of certain professions, something most of us learn once we're out in the workplace.

STEREOTYPES CONNECT — BUT USE THEM WITH CAUTION

Stereotyping is slightly more risky humour than either of the first two types I've mentioned. Use it sparingly and with caution because once in a while someone will take offense to the idea of stereotypes, or to the particular stereotype you are using. They work best when you are speaking to a group with a strong identity of its own and refer to a contrasting but equally well-defined group. Students of one university will laugh at students from another; citizens of my tiny hometown enjoy jokes about a smaller, less sophisticated town nearby, and one professional group will jokingly target another; all examples of using humour through stereotyping to connect with an audience.

Sonny Bono, when first elected Congressman, used both self-deprecating humour and stereotyping to ease his way onto Capitol Hill where he wasn't widely respected due to his earlier career as an entertainer. Speaking to the Washington Press Club Foundation shortly after taking office in January 1995, Bono said, *"The last thing in the world I thought I would be is a U.S. congressman, given all the bobcat vests and Eskimo boots I used to wear. I love this game. I am so pleased that we are all so dedicated to mankind — unlike show business, where you have egomaniacs and you have power mongers and you have elitists."* His audience is reported[7] to have, *"...roared... and the initial scorn began to crumble."*

TAKE DIRECT AIM AT YOUR AUDIENCE — IF YOU KNOW THEM WELL

There is a fourth type of humour you may have noticed in the example from Bono's maiden address. He poked fun, albeit indirectly, at his audience of politicians. This can be dangerous but because he was so indirect, and because his audience would be used to far sharper criticism, it was hardly a gamble at all. As speakers we can certainly gamble by teasing an audience if we are pretty sure they would find it funny.

In a Toastmasters Club, where the goal is to help participants build self-esteem, every participant is applauded for even a minimal performance. Members know this response is amusing to non-members and quite enjoy being teased about their willingness to *"applaud anything."* An outsider who mentions this will generate laughter and immediately connect with the club members.

This ability to connect by tapping into another group's culture can be fun to observe. The Rotary clubs I've attended seemed always to be fining each other for infractions: a dollar for telling a joke, a couple of dollars if the joke is political, five dollars if you appear on television or have something published in the local paper and, when the member's birthday rolls around, an even larger fine calculated on age. This is all done with much laughter, and the money collected is used to support various Rotary charities. A non-member can usually raise a chortle by commenting on the fines, perhaps by saying, *"At the risk of attracting attention from your Sergeant at Arms, and incurring a steep fine...."* Rotarians have a delightful sense of humour about themselves and are therefore willing to take some teasing by a speaker.

By contrast, credit unions in my area did an advertising campaign in which they attacked the large chartered banks and labelled them, "Humungous Bank." The advertisements, which were hilarious in their exaggeration, were widely played on local media and appeared in print form. The chartered banks were not amused, and although no banks were specifically named, they sought to have the campaign terminated. A speaker talking to an audience from one of the chartered banks would not have connected with the group by teasing them about any aspect of this campaign because, amusing as it was to the non-banking community, it was hurtful to the banks and their dedicated employees.

CASH IN ON UNEXPECTED FUN

Audience knowledge and careful thought are important in selecting all humour. However, often the best humour, but also the riskiest humour, comes from something that happens spontaneously while you are performing. One speaker got an excellent response when a waiter dropped a tray of coffee cups forcing him to stop talking. When the noise of breaking crockery finally subsided, he got his audience to give the waiter a standing ovation. The audience loved it; the waiter bowed, clasped his hands over his head in a victory salute, and the speech went on. Perhaps one or two members of that audience might have been offended at a speaker taking advantage of a powerless waiter, but the rest of the audience saw the humour in this most human of situations.

Another speaker, using an overhead projector in a small conference room in the Napa Valley, suddenly had a very large fly appear on his screen. It performed little fly push-ups which were projected onto the screen as enormous fly push-ups. The speaker stopped, stood back and admired the insect, remarked on its amazing level of fitness, and then told it to go get its own stage; this was his and he wasn't sharing. By then everyone was chortling. This was totally safe humour unless there happened to be someone in the audience worrying about the dignity of flies.

TEASING IS FUN, BUT TOO OFTEN IT HURTS SOMEONE

Teasing audience members is a great deal more risky than picking on insects. I once gave a speech about nail biting. I didn't immediately identify what vice I'd be discussing; in fact, I thought it would be funnier if I implied it was a habit hardly ever discussed in polite society and one that involved a lot of sucking and slurping noises. (Use your imagination here, my audience certainly did.) On the spur of the moment, just before identifying the topic, I noticed a fellow with very short nails and the puffy red cuticles that accompany excessive nail munching and said, "*I think Joey*[8] *indulges in this habit too and like me he probably hides out, behind closed doors, enjoying his forbidden pleasure.*" This fellow was known for his own funny speeches, and I assumed he'd have a great sense of humour about this topic too. And he did, until it became apparent I was talking about nail biting. Then he blushed with intense embarrassment. In my attempt to get a laugh, I'd hurt a member of the audience. Others realized his discomfort, and rather than connecting me to my audience, I drove a wedge into the group. So, when your humour is targeted at another person or group, be very sure they'll be as amused as you are. If you haven't seen evidence that they find the topic laughable, avoid using it.

CAN JOKES CONNECT YOU TO AN AUDIENCE?

Many speakers use jokes in their presentations, and although I don't use them a lot anymore, I certainly think they are useful. Jokes have a couple of disadvantages. It's hard to find one that isn't known to at least some of your audience. Also, they tend to be generic rather than personalized to the audience. And if they bomb, unlike other types of humour it's hard to pretend you weren't trying to be funny. But jokes can help a speaker gain audience acceptance early in a speech, and if carefully chosen, edited, and performed, can add a lot.

If you do use jokes, avoid informing the audience you are about to tell one. For some strange reason this seems to create a set of expectations that are difficult to fulfill. It's almost as if the audience is sitting there, arms crossed, saying, *"go ahead, sucker, make me laugh!"* If you can slip into the anecdote without indicating it is a joke, if you keep the build-up brief, and if it is an appropriate joke for the audience and the situation, you'll get a great response even though they know they've been had. How you blend back into your speech is just as important. Sometimes the punchline will slide nicely into your next message, but sometimes you have to connect your joke to your speech after the laughter has subsided.

"I once heard a story about two ants on a golf course." As soon you hear the opening line you know it is a joke and are intrigued by the image. In this joke, the ants are too close to an unskilled golfer who takes a whack at the ball, misses it, but sends the ants and the clod of dirt they were standing on down the golf course. This scene is repeated twice.[9] Finally, after three tumultuous flights, one ant turns to the other and says, *"You know, if we're going to survive, I think we'd better get on the ball."* Here is a brief joke with a punchline that leads immediately to a statement such as, *"…and if we're going to survive, here at International Impressive Conglomerate Bank, we'd better get on the ball too."* Not all jokes offer such an easy segue back to your speech, but you do need to find adequate transitions.

Sometimes you can ease into a joke by pretending the story happened to you. I rarely tell humorous bear stories anymore but I used to have a whole series of them. Some were in fact stories from my own days as a camper and hiker; others were jokes I found in various books. When I began a bear story my audience wasn't ever quite sure if this was one from my real life or a planned joke. This added an element of surprise, which as I pointed out, accounts for much of the potential success of humour. But I also needed to find a way to connect the final joke to the remainder of my speech.

After two previous references to my camping experiences, I told about being chased downhill by a bear. At the bottom of the hill there was a wide stream, but with the motivation provided by that angry mamma bear, I took the leap of my lifetime and cleared the stream, only to fall face down in deep mud on the riverbank. Before I could get myself out of the mud, that mamma bear was upon me. I could feel her hot breath on the back of my neck as she prepared for her human feast. I did what anyone would have done in that situation, I prayed. *"Lord, Lord – please give this bear religion."* And to my amazement, a shaft of light came down from heaven and fastened on that bear's forehead. She sat upright, folded her big shaggy paws, bowed her head and said, *"For what I am about to receive, make me truly grateful."* My transition statement is, *"And I hope you'll be grateful for what you are about to receive in this speech."* If the audience isn't immediately aware that a joke is being told, they certainly are by the end. With the exception of the dental surgeon noted in the previous chapter, I've had a good response to this playful way of saying I aim to please them.

VISUALLY ENTERTAIN THEM TO CONNECT

While many of the techniques I've suggested are unplanned and incidental humour, jokes fall into the category of planned humour. Likewise, a sixth type, visual humour, falls into this category. Some speakers create or use cartoons to add humour. I've seen several speakers create a lot of mirth simply by projecting amusing headlines, advertisements, and quotations. Some speakers can perform a little magic or use costumes to add humour. A Washington-based speaker, Silvana Clark,[10] in her speech about involving the audience, ended the program with her young daughter appearing from a trunk. This certainly went off the charts on the element of surprise and it won major laughter from her audience.

One of my favourite examples of a visual used to connect speaker, audience, and idea was used by the fitness director in a large company. In speaking to new recruits, she urged them to set some health and fitness goals for themselves and let her programs help them achieve those goals. She mentioned weight loss as a possible goal and asked the audience if any of them had ever wanted to lose five or ten pounds of extra weight. With prompting, quite a few employees indicated they had.

She said losing five extra pounds in the next few months was certainly a worthy goal, and it was important to be able to visualize that goal. Next she held up a previously hidden food model representing five pounds of ugly fat. It was made of that soft, oily-feeling plastic commonly seen in slimy children's toys, and it was a hideous yellow colour. If you've ever seen little globs of yellow fat on raw chicken, you have some idea of what the audience was seeing, except this was five pounds of the stuff, so imagine something about the size of a football.

There was an audible reaction, including laughter and remarks such as, *"O-oh, gross!"*, to the food model. After the murmuring died down, she reminded them it was important to visualize a goal, and it would be helpful if they could each touch the model, hold it in their hands, and feel its weight and composition in an effort to have a memorable image available when they needed it. As they had a coffee break coming up, she said she'd make it available then. In fact, in order to help them she'd place it *"…over here, right beside the cookies and coffee."* They howled.

There was a third round of laughter when, at coffee break, the five pounds of ugly fat was circulated while they ate their cookies and put sugar into their coffee. I can't promise they all took up her challenge, but I do know she used her visual well in adding humour that let her connect with her audience and make her point memorable.

Using visuals and props to create humour takes some planning and rehearsal, but it's often well received by an audience and therefore worth the effort. When Dr. Martha Piper, Ph.D.,[11] took office as President of British Columbia's largest and oldest university (UBC), she wanted to issue a strong message that change was on the way. She wanted to signal it to the students, the employees, and the business and professional communities. She appeared in business dress but early in the presentation donned a baseball cap emblazoned with the slogan, "THinK About It", that won the laughter and attention she wanted. Laughter at the unusual academic costume grew as the audience began to put on matching caps. It might not be right for you in your next business address, but it certainly worked for this university president.

One of my clients, while delivering a business proposal, incorporated a phone call to add humour. She used her child's bright blue princess phone to role play a hilarious version of their firm's worst nightmare. Corporate executives laughed and subsequently committed most of a million dollars to her customer service proposal. Not everyone is willing to try props or costumes to make a point with humour, but if done tastefully the yield can be great.

In a team presentation urging a large retail firm to customize its sales approach based on information collected and stored in a specialized database, one member of the team took on the role of customer.

Initially he was just a mystery client wearing an appropriate Zorro type mask. Later, as his interests were identified, he pulled on an oversized cowboy hat, picked up his cellular phone and laptop computer, and put on an enormous gold wedding ring. With these props in place, his team used him periodically to discuss his response to their proposal from the perspective of the client. When they promised to remind him of his wedding anniversary, keep him updated on the latest computer games, and let him know when new shipments of western wear would first hit the stores, he responded very positively. This minor part of the team's business proposal had a huge impact on the executive team assembled. No decision was made that day (nor was it expected), but following the formal presentation the executives were on their feet mingling with the presenters and asking many additional questions. This team definitely used humour effectively to connect.

You can't keep all of the people happy all of the time

As I've said repeatedly, not all humour is safe. Avoid anything that will make you or your audience uncomfortable, but don't avoid humour on the basis that someone somewhere won't like it. You are bound to come across someone who is overly sensitive to almost everything that other people find amusing.

My husband tells a very funny story about an encounter with his ex-wife several years after they were divorced. It in no way denigrates his former partner, and it is a tasteful story where the sudden appearance of his former spouse is essential to the humour. He used it in a speech recently, to the great amusement of his audience, but after the speech one member of the audience approached him to say how inappropriate it was to mention his former wife in this way. I'm not sure what baggage this woman might have, but I certainly wouldn't recommend ditching the story simply because of a single woman's response to it.

When attending meetings together, my husband and I often tease each other publicly. Speaking to a group that knows us both well, I related an amusing incident where he could have saved a lot of time by reading directions – even if he never read anything else. This is a group who knows he isn't a great reader and also knows I'm arithmetically challenged, to the extent that they refer to me as "Words" and my husband as "Numbers."

The next day I got one of those, *"I don't like what you just did"* phone calls. According to my critic I had damaged my husband's self-esteem with my story. I certainly think it's worth examining the anecdote and deciding if it needs adjustment or should be purged from my speaking file, but if most of the audience enjoyed the material and it helped forge a connection, I wouldn't eliminate it based on one person's negative response.

In every audience of any size there is likely to be someone who will be a little uncomfortable with your humour. Perhaps this is human nature or perhaps society's emphasis on human rights and political correctness has caused a few people to overreact. Of course a speaker needs to use caution and of course a speaker needs to avoid dealing with sensitive topics in an overly jolly way, but avoiding humour altogether hardly seems to be the answer. In fact there are situations where injecting some laughter feels like the only way to deal with the topic.

Attending the funeral of a friend who had died too young and suddenly, leaving a number of children in their early adult years, I was impressed by his brother's ability to relate an amusing anecdote during the eulogy.

The family lived in an upscale neighbourhood close to a major river where nearby sawmills still produce huge piles of wood chips and sawdust. My friend was walking with his youngest daughter when they noticed a bench had been set in concrete and dedicated to a local family. His daughter, with no idea her father would soon die, asked, *"Dad, after you die, if we dedicate a bench to you here by the river, what inscription would you like on the plaque?"* According to his brother, the father's response was, *"In memory of our father. He loved the smell of sawdust."* There may have been a few people who thought his comments irreverent, but the large church reverberated with joy. We felt connected in celebration of the life of a dear friend.

DEVELOP YOUR FUNNY BONE TO CONNECT

Humour is a powerful tool for connecting with your audience that is well worth developing. You can improve your use of humour in several ways. Watch other speakers, and when they get a positive reaction, try to record what was said and then analyze why it might have worked. Watch the audience for signs of bonding; not every laugh signals a strong connection between the audience and the speaker.

To determine your own favourite types of humour, read amusing material, listen to humorists on radio programs or tapes, and watch comedic performances. For example, if you wanted to learn how to handle jokes that bomb, watch tapes of Johnny Carson on the Tonight Show. He often got better laughs for his saving lines than for his initial jokes. You can learn a great deal by observing others.

After you've seen or heard someone use good humorous material, try it out yourself. It's unlikely you'll ever use someone else's material without adjusting it anyway, but the practice of delivering humour will build your skills and confidence. When you observe and practice retelling other people's jokes, pay attention to the pattern of pauses used. Most humour incorporates a pause just before the punchline to signal the audience they are about to hear the funny part. Another pause follows the punchline so the audience will have an opportunity to laugh.

EXERCISE YOUR FUNNY BONE

I was once asked if I thought speakers who used humour effectively were born that way. I don't believe they are. Speakers who tell jokes well tell more jokes than the rest of us. They also bomb more than the rest of us. Speakers who use comedy in their presentations simply realize they need it and start incorporating it into their presentations. I'm sure most of them have had their share of disasters and near disasters with humour, but they've persevered, and by the time we see them they just seem to have a natural talent for being funny. So, start using humour in your least important presentations and gradually you'll find you can incorporate it into all types of speaking. You'll enjoy your audiences more, they'll enjoy you more, and someday, somewhere, someone will come up to you after you speak and tell you they think you were born funny. You can say, *"I don't know about that, I'll have to ask my Mom."*, or you can politely thank them for the great compliment.

SUMMARY: USE HUMOUR TO CONNECT

• Make sure it's appropriate to the audience and situation.

• Laugh at yourself but maintain your dignity.

• Be brief (unless you are delivering an entertaining speech).

• Deliver humour well, with a pause before the punchline and a pause afterwards to let the audience enjoy it.

Notes

1 Dr. Charles Jarvis, "Humor Workshop" Toastmasters International Convention, August 19, 1981. Dr. Jarvis practiced dentistry for twelve years before starting his professional speaking career in 1959.

2 Douglas Anderson, President of D.D. Anderson and Associates, a life insurance firm, has been a member of Toastmasters since 1969.

3 John Nichols, "Narrow Gauge Railways of Great Britain," 14th National Garden Railway Conference, 1997.

4 John Nichols, "Narrow Gauge Railways of Great Britain," 14th National Garden Railway Conference, 1997.

5 Judy Johnson, President of Johnson, Hall and Associates, a consulting firm specializing in management training and speaking.

6 Rotary Youth Leadership Award – a 3-4 day residential program to increase voluntary leadership skills in the delegates who are 18 – 25 years of age.

7 As reported by Matt Fitzsimmons in the Desert Sun, *The Sonny Side of the House,* January 7, 1998.

8 Definitely not his real name!

9 A common structure for jokes is threes. I've heard it described by comedy writer, Gene Perret, as two straights and a curve, the curve being the funny part of the joke.

10 Sylvana Clark, Luncheon Address, "It's A Jungle Out There!", June 21, 1996, Seattle, WA.

11 Martha Piper, Inauguration Address, Chan Center, University of British Columbia, September 25, 1997.

CHAPTER 8

INVOLVE YOUR AUDIENCE TO CONNECT

ONE OF THE MOST OBVIOUS WAYS TO CONNECT WITH AN AUDIENCE IS TO involve them through some type of participation in your speech or presentation. This can be very simple, such as a show-of-hands response, or quite complex, such as in games, role-plays, and simulation activities. Every type of presentation can incorporate audience participation, but your choice of activity will depend on variables such as available time, objectives, setting and, of course, listeners. A role-play in which participants play out customer complaints is well suited to a training presentation where plenty of time is available for preparation, performance, evaluation, and discussion. It would be a poor choice for a ten-minute team strategy session or a keynote address. And, in many cases, the value of the interaction is in how you deliver it rather than in any intrinsic sense.

SIMPLE RESPONSES CONNECT

Asking the audience to indicate their responses is a fine way to elicit participation. Speakers often ask for a show of hands, but most participants will also welcome the chance to stand briefly, if only because it lets them stretch. You can also invite them to nod, smile, wave, or cheer in response.

One speaker instructed his audience to pick up their programs, fold them vertically, and set them up on the seminar tables in front of them. He asked the participants to lower them to the table when he touched on any subject of special interest. Some lowered them very quickly, others didn't indicate their special interest until very late in his program. This small activity provided useful feedback for the speaker, who capitalized on it by remembering who had lowered their program at a certain point and referring to them when he summarized his remarks. The activity definitely connected speaker to audience, and they stayed attentive throughout his speech.

Another speaker[1] at a presentation I attended asked us to stand if the following statement described us: *"I am a secondary school teacher."* Perhaps twenty people stood; the speaker took a moment to look them over, thank them, and invite them to sit. Next he had the elementary teachers and the administrators stand. Not fitting any of these categories, I was feeling a little left out until, after an impish grin and a slight pause, our speaker gave us one more opportunity to identify ourselves with the description: *"I am hopelessly addicted to chocolate."* I leapt to my feet, happy to be included.

This type of participation was simple; it didn't use a lot of time and it gave the speaker useful information. It might have served to segment the audience, but because of the fourth statement it got us laughing instead. He placed this activity right at the beginning of his presentation, thus paving the way for further interaction. This very brief participation established an initial connection with his audience.

By contrast, consider the speaker who asked for a show of hands in answer to the questions: *"How many of you are from this city?"*, *"How many of you are from somewhere else in the province?"*, and *"How many of you are from somewhere outside this province?"* There was a lackluster response to her questions, at least in part because she wasn't paying attention to the group and didn't insist on participation. She barely noted where hands went up, didn't in any way acknowledge the responses, and without any transition began to talk about changes in the healthcare delivery system. Her questions were relevant to this content, because the impact of her remarks would vary depending on where her audience lived, yet she missed the opportunity to connect with her audience and to connect them to her subject.

IT TAKES MORE THAN A VERBAL REQUEST TO CONNECT

The show-of-hands technique is quite useful as an opening but only if you give it full delivery. When I speak about body language, I often begin by asking the audience to take a stand, to identify their beliefs about the subject. First I ask, *"How many of you believe — let's have a show of hands – how many of you believe your own body language is affecting your career success?"* After asking the question I raise my own hand to model the response I want and simultaneously look at the audience to encourage their participation. Most participants raise their hands, so I reinforce my interest by saying, *"It seems like most of us believe our body language influences our careers."* My second question is similar but related to success with family and friends. I don't need the verbal prompt but I still use eye contact, raise my own hand (as a believer), and acknowledge the even larger level of agreement.

My third question is about their intimate relations. This generates laughter and almost everyone raises their hands when I raise mine. After a brief pause I ask my final question. *"How many of you are getting tired of raising your hands?"* There are always a few who raise their hands out of habit and as a response to my body language prompt, but then realizing what I've asked, dissolve into laughter. Some hold their hands even higher and make direct eye contact signalling me that they are indeed tired of the hand-raising. I take a moment to thank them for playing along with me and then connect the activity to the value we all place on body language.

This opening didn't work perfectly the first time I tried it, but as I learned to ask for exactly what I wanted, model the action I wanted, look at the audience as I asked, and wait until they complied, I began to get the results I wanted. I wanted to connect with them but also to connect them to the topic and their own beliefs about the subject. The fourth question is completely off-topic but injects a little humour into the silliness of raising your hands in public. It lets us laugh at the human condition and thus further serves to connect us.

Caution!

I've had speakers tell me they avoid hand-raising and other interactions because the audience doesn't like it. And to some extent they are correct. If the speaker uses any technique too much, if the technique is poorly introduced or simply a gratuitous interaction, if the audience and setting are very formal, or if the interaction embarrasses anyone, the audiences won't like hand-raising and other methods to engage their participation.

One speaker had us stand and introduce ourselves to the person behind us. Logistically this didn't work, so there was mass confusion, some laughter, and plenty of noise with several hundred delegates speaking at once. In my opinion it wasn't a strong choice because the speaker in no way connected this self-introduction to anything he was saying. But the next speaker was even worse. She had us stand up and hug the person seated next to us. I don't hug strangers, so I voted with my feet and went to the women's restroom. That area quickly filled with disgruntled participants who felt hugging was nonsensical at a business seminar with a time management theme.

Hand-raising has some definite limitations. I was the eighth speaker in a weekly business training program and my audience, primarily from car dealerships, hadn't chosen to take the program. The owners of the dealerships instructed them to attend and learn how to operate their businesses more productively. If you're getting the feeling I wasn't speaking to the most enthusiastic of audiences, you are correct in that assumption.

I had used a hands-up activity at the start of the three-hour seminar and they willingly participated, but about an hour into the program I asked the audience to again respond by raising their hands. Before anyone could respond, a man near the front asked, *"Why do all you business types think we want to keep raising our hands?"* Someone else quickly backed him up by saying, *"Yeah, every speaker we've had has made us raise our hands all evening. Is that the only way you guys know how to give a speech?"* I hadn't seen the other speakers, so I'd walked into it with blinders on, but their criticism was fair and served to remind me that even the best technique is worthless, sometimes counterproductive, if overused or poorly chosen for the audience. Interaction techniques have the power to connect you to an audience, but they also have the power to irritate and annoy.

Another audience interaction technique that certainly infuriates many intelligent listeners is one used by motivational speakers. Instead of notes, they offer a one-page handout containing unfinished statements such as, *"Success is ____% inspiration and ____% perspiration."* The blanks are words, slogans, and statistics the listeners are supposed to fill in on command. The audience is involved in an activity, but there isn't much bonding happening because the speaker and the audience aren't engaged in any interaction. If you use this activity, use it sparingly and consider that few adults like to be told exactly what to do and when to do it.

BE CREATIVE TO CONNECT THROUGH INTERACTION

Seeking a wider variety of audience participation techniques and using your own creativity will do a great deal to improve your presentation.

The following examples show some creative ways speakers can use audience participation to forge a strong bond.

Imagine yourself in a high-level audience of perhaps fifteen decision makers. The speaker, Anne, is from one of Canada's First Nations groups, and while junior to all of you in her audience, has made significant contributions in the few months she has worked for your agency. She has been making a supreme effort to sensitize all of you to the special concerns of native groups and has slowly won recognition for her insights and support for her recommendations.

Anne begins her presentation by laying a beautiful blanket over a small table and asks each member of the audience to give her something of value. The first gentleman offers her the keys to his Lexus. She accepts them reverently and places them carefully on her ritual table. The next woman slips off her gold necklace which is also laid on the table. You are next. You reach into your wallet and select your most impressive credit card. But Anne rejects it; she wants you to offer something of real value. The audience gently laughs and several others re-evaluate their offerings. After several tries she accepts the worn photo of your child. A gold watch, a wallet molded to the posterior of its owner, a time management notebook, a laptop computer, and one Gucci loafer are added to the table. Anne gives her attention briefly to each audience member as she accepts their offerings and decorously places them on her blanket. She thanks them for their contributions and promises to return to them later.

Like any good speaker, Anne now previews her proposal and quickly moves into her points, supporting each with stories, examples, gentle humour, and factual information. She invites you to ask questions and voice your concerns regarding her proposal, and after successfully handling objections, Anne moves into her close. She has used fifteen minutes of your time and has asked support for a new approach to handling immunization in remote native communities. If not full approval, she has won your support to move to the next level of investigation on this issue. Closure seems imminent.

Suddenly, your agency chief remembers the keys to his Lexus are still on her blanketed table, and Anne has made no mention of them nor any move to return them. Exerting his leadership, he inquires about the purpose of the table and the objects of value. You sense a collective holding of breaths around you as the audience expects to hear the meaning of such a ceremony. Anne pauses, grins widely, and says, *"Oh, that. I just wanted you to stay through until I finished my proposal, and I was worried you wouldn't unless you had invested something of value in the presentation.*" This evokes relieved laughter in the group and increases her acceptance and level of respect in the agency. She has connected using audience participation.

Few of us would ever use this particular activity, yet we can learn from her skillful audience participation technique. I was in Anne's audience and greatly admired her skill. She played on her cultural heritage by bringing the blanket and ceremoniously laying it over a table to receive our gifts. This established a mysterious, almost mystical feeling in the room. She then asked for our valuables and with only one correction was able to get items of distinct value from us. As she accepted each gift she was required to interact with each member of her audience, and since we were also required to interact with her, we couldn't ignore the person speaking to us. She wasn't simply a someone making a funding request; she was Anne, interacting closely with us.

Once she had established the feeling and the connection, Anne had our attention and our respect. The ceremonial gift giving was a ruse, yet we didn't mind because we had great pleasure from it. In fact, the punchline gave us an opportunity to relate to each other on a more relaxed basis, thus ending the formal relationship and establishing a congenial atmosphere for the continued discussion of the immunization program and other important matters. Anne not only reached her immediate goal, she also built a relationship with her audience. It will be hard to ignore her in future decision making because Anne has proven herself not only as a thinker and a doer, but also as a warm humanitarian with a fine sense of humour.

Although you've likely seen platform speakers use interaction, you can see the value of audience interaction even in a formal governmental meeting where a proposal was being made to a high-level audience. Another audience interaction technique I've seen used in small audiences of this nature was set up before the session.

In this example, the speaker was addressing other department heads about a change in her department, a change they would need to support in order to save their hospital a considerable amount of money. She feared her audience would stonewall her, and that the change wouldn't get due consideration let alone approval. She knew the Chief Financial Officer (CFO), who would represent the administration department, had the most to gain by supporting her. In an earlier private meeting with this person, they had reviewed concerns from some other departments and built a strategy together. When the speaker laid out her proposal and called for questions, the room was silent, exactly as she expected. Enter the CFO who, right on cue, addressed the head of emergency services personally and said, *"Yvonne, weren't you concerned about the cost of training for this change? You and I were talking about that on Monday."* Yvonne looked a bit surprised at first but suddenly began airing her concerns which got everyone into the fray. The proposal got full discussion, and the department heads eventually approved a carefully amended plan. Planned interaction created the connection in this business speech.

The previous examples have used minimal interaction to achieve their purpose, but sometimes an entire presentation is shaped around interaction. Autumn Scraper,[2] addressing the business of Pensions and Benefits Consulting at a Human Resources conference, showed her peers, myself included, how to bring their information to a non-expert audience. She first divided participants into eight teams. Using the general rules of the television game show, Jeopardy!, we were to select categories and try to be the first team to give the correct answers. Each team had an audible signal to let the judges know they wanted to answer first. Using a fairly primitive multimedia system, we selected topics from the list, and after attempting an answer, were given the correct answer and more detail. Detail varied from slides and cartoons to full video clips, and each was interesting and unique. Autumn's personal delivery enhanced the connections in this program too. She used plenty of humour to keep the group amused, called many participants by their names, complimented individuals and teams for their creative answers, had prizes for the winning teams, and stayed afterwards to talk with the curious and the well-wishers, of which there were many since Autumn had so admirably won their approval.

GAMES AND ACTIVITIES CAN HELP YOU CONNECT

Games rarely become the entire focus of a presentation although adjusting popular games is certainly a way to achieve audience participation. Competition can cause some people to disengage, but in Autumn's case the style and purpose of her session were well advertised to the conference registrants and her session was wait-listed. She made the situation less threatening by having us perform on teams, and anonymity was further enhanced by dimming the lights for the multimedia. The awards at the end of her program were blatant advertising for her company, a factor that could have been a negative, but the audience was so supportive that all I heard was a little good-natured teasing. In fact I heard one of her competitor's remark about the high-quality sweatshirts with more than passing envy. Autumn's session represented her well, it reflected well on her firm, and it connected.

Games and activities can also be used briefly, yet effectively, in presentations. On two separate occasions I've seen speakers use a quick participation game as a way to introduce the theme of change. Participants were first asked to find a partner and stand facing one another. They were then instructed to take a good look at each other. After about a minute, they were instructed to turn away from each other and change three things about their appearance. Amidst plenty of giggling, clothing was rearranged, jewelry, shoes, and belts came off. Partners were to face each other again and try to determine the changes. Next they were instructed to face away again and change seven more things about their appearance. Almost immediately there was a terrible rumbling in the audience because changing three things was easy, but making so many additional changes was hard. The activity was suspended and the participants, giggling while they dressed themselves again, took their seats. Both speakers remarked that extensive change is hard on people, and we shouldn't forget this principle in planning change.

The preceding exercise connected participants to each other and provided an effective lead into the topic. Activities such as this where participants interact without the leader don't always forge strong speaker-listener connections, but have value in that they establish an environment of participation such that any further requests from the speaker will likely get strong compliance.

I sometimes use brief theater games to help business and professional clients take a fresh look at interpersonal communications. I'll usually demonstrate the game with a couple of volunteers, which teaches the activity and gives me an opportunity to bond with my audience. These activities work for me in keynotes and seminars but they'd be a poor choice in a boardroom presentation or a very formal address.

Asking participants to guess or estimate a figure is a way to bring participation into a business presentation. The chief of staff at a hospital used this technique in a series of presentations to government, employees, and the community. He gave them current costs, outlined operational changes giving the savings for each change, and asked them to predict the final savings. His audiences tended to sum the savings of each change and arrive at an acceptable figure just over a quarter of a million dollars. He then gave them the real answer which was much closer to a half million in savings. He'd gotten them involved, he'd connected, and now he had their attention as he showed them how each change, when combined with the others, created a much greater saving; the whole was greater than the parts. This minor interaction with his audience helped the chief of staff win support for his initiatives and forged strong relationships with his various constituents.

USE INTERACTION EARLY; YOUR AUDIENCE WILL PARTICIPATE MORE READILY

Whether participation is extensive as in the mock *Jeopardy!* game show or a simple small interaction such as a request for the audience to guess at a final figure, it works to connect speaker, topic, and audience. But, even knowing its value, I've still found speakers who avoid anything involving audience participation for fear they'll have to deal with the results. It's true that once you get participants talking, moving, and interacting they do require a bit more management.

I used to do negotiation seminars as part of a government project to provide business skills upgrades for owners and managers of small businesses. I always delivered my seminar about eight to ten months into the program with only the vaguest idea of what the other seven or eight presenters had said or done. Believing they already knew a lot about the topic and would learn more through interaction and discussion, I always had the participants actually negotiate three cases. They really enjoyed themselves, and periodically a participant or a program manager would remark how it was the first time he or she had seen the group really interacting. Apparently group interaction was one of the goals of the program, a goal no one had figured out how to address.

After a year or two I was invited to develop the opening seminar for this program. I was to address the subject of networking and to get participants interacting with each other. It turned out to be quite an easy task as they readily interacted with me and with each other once they were given specific directions and told this was part of their program. The problem came when we tried to get them to stop interacting, a delightful problem in my opinion. However, one of the program advisors told me he wasn't sure he wanted me to keynote his next program. Apparently he'd had trouble getting them to sit down and listen at the start of the subsequent seminars, and the other speakers were complaining about the highly interactive behaviour of the participants. It's difficult to believe anyone would choose a passive audience over an active and engaged one, but I suppose there are speakers who would find it distressing.

If you are still resisting the idea of interaction, think back to the communication cycle introduced in Chapter 1. The more interactive you are with your listener, the more likely you are to get their verbal and non-verbal feedback, thus completing the cycle of communication. The more passive your audience, the more difficult it will be to sense audience needs, interests, and concerns. Interaction helps us get the audience information we need to make the best choices as we speak.

SUMMARY: INVOLVE YOUR AUDIENCE TO CONNECT

- Use participation early to establish the expectation.
- Give clear directions so participants know what they are to perform or do.
- Model the behaviour if you can – for "hands-up", raise your own hand.
- Insist on participation – give directions, look at them, await their response.
- Reward participation – it could be tangibles, but even thanking the audience or ending with humour makes most participants glad they participated.
- Connect the participation to the content of your presentation.

Notes

[1] Robert J. Garmston, "How to Make Presentations That Teach and Transform", Vancouver, BC, August 28, 1995. In his book, *How to Make Presentations That Teach and Transform* (Association for Supervision and Curriculum Development, Alexandria, VA, 1992), Garmston refers to this as a "Just Like Me" opener.

[2] Autumn Scaper, Coles Group, addressing the HRMA in May 1996.

CHAPTER 9

USE WORDS TO CONNECT

PERHAPS THE SIMPLEST WAY TO CONNECT IS THROUGH WORD CHOICES. Whether you are speaking to a few people or to an enormous audience, whether delivering a motivational address or a business report, whether seated or standing, using visuals or simply talking, well-chosen words can help you forge a bond with your listener.

When American President, John F. Kennedy, delivered his famous inaugural address,[1] he did not say, *"People should ask not what the country can do but what can be done for this country."* He said, *"And so, my fellow Americans: ask not what your country can do for you — ask what you can do for your country."* British Prime Minister, Sir Winston Churchill,[2] did not say, *"The soldiers will fight on the beaches. The soldiers will fight on the landing grounds. They shall fight in the fields, and in the streets, they shall fight in the hills."* He said, *"We shall fight on the beaches. We shall fight on the landing grounds. We shall fight in the fields and in the streets, we shall fight in the hills. We shall never surrender!"* These speakers won attention and support because they used words powerfully to connect them to their audiences.

PERSONAL PRONOUNS ARE POWERFUL CONNECTORS

In each case, they used personal pronouns. *You* and *your* are useful when you want the audience to think and respond as individuals. Kennedy chose this approach in making all citizens feel they should take personal responsibility for the future of their nation. *We, our,* and *us* are useful when you want to include yourself as part of the audience. Churchill wanted the British people to feel the power of belonging to a proud and courageous nation protecting itself against a strong enemy.

When you speak you can use these five personal pronouns to help your audience feel you are speaking about them. Instead of saying, *"People sometimes notice...",* use you; *"You might have noticed...",* or instead of *"That's not within the school boundary,"* use our; *"...not within our school boundary."* Likewise, *"We're all going to benefit from this approach...",* is more personal than, *"This approach is beneficial because...",* and *"You've seen this before...",* connects better than *"This has been presented before...."* Whenever you need to connect with your audience, look for opportunities to personalize your message with personal pronouns.

AVOID PERSONAL PRONOUNS IF...

There are reasons to avoid personal pronouns. Avoid them if in using them you are being dishonest. When a speaker uses *we* but means *I,* that speaker is being dishonest. For example, if your speaker was a consultant working independently of others, and said, *"We are always here to serve you,"* the speaker is using the pronoun to suggest that a sizable firm gives service to your account. Since you know it isn't true, as a listener you'd quite reasonably feel the speaker is being dishonest. As a speaker, it isn't a wise deception.

You might also choose to avoid personal pronouns when discussing negative ideas, assuming you aren't wanting to point the finger at anyone. *"Absenteeism has created a problem at this time,"* is certainly less accusatory than *"Some of you have high levels of absenteeism."* Sometimes switching from *you* and *your* to *we, our,* and *us,* softens the message sufficiently. *"Absenteeism has created a problem for us. We all need to be vigilant about our use of sick-leave and personal days."* As with all the choices you'll make in an effort to connect, you have to keep thinking of your audience. Ask yourself how you'd feel if you were listening to this use of personal pronouns.

PROPER NOUNS ARE VALUABLE CONNECTORS

You can further add warmth to your speech and develop rapport with your audience by using proper nouns. For example, if you were addressing the members of the Armstrong Spallumcheen Museum and Arts Society,[3] you could say, *"Here in Armstrong/Spallumcheen, where your summers are warm and welcoming...."* By using the name of their city and municipality, you demonstrate your awareness of who they are. If you were from the area, you could stress your involvement by using *our* in place of *your:"Here in Armstrong / Spallumcheen, where our summers are warm and welcoming...."* You can use the names of participants or others they'd know. *"Your President, Mrs. Hamilton, was unable to be here today, but she told me...."* You've used a familiar name and indicated you've made contact with her prior to the meeting. If I was in your audience, I'd feel pleased to know you'd cared enough to do some research before addressing us.

You can even incorporate names of people you've just met. Suppose Mary met you at the door and showed you to the speaking area, you could thank her in your opening by saying, *"I thank you for inviting me to your city, and a special thanks to Mary, who so graciously welcomed me when I arrived."*

If you hear the speaker say your name, you'll probably sit up a little straighter and pay a bit more attention. Hearing your name from the speaker, combined with some type of non-verbal acknowledgment, such as a wink or a brief hand gesture, also makes you feel included. And even if you don't hear your own name, you get the feeling the speaker is aware of you and your companions.

CAUTION! THERE'S SUCH A THING AS OVERKILL

A word of caution on using people's names is probably in order here. If you've ever had a salesperson learn your name and use it in every sentence, you already know that overusing one person's name is irritating for all. *"Henry, what you need to know, Henry, is that this frog is better than all others on the market. Now I know, Henry, you're probably thinking I'm wrong, that your current frog is just fine but, Henry, if I can show you this frog will jump farther than any frog you've ever seen...."* Overuse of a name is a sales killer whether in direct sales or speechmaking. Use a variety of names so as many people as possible are included, and don't overuse the technique.

Apply this recommendation to any other proper noun you might use. For example, the name customers use for their product would be a wise addition but not if you overused it. Suppose your client makes models for training physicians and first aid attendants, you could refer to the product by its full name, *"Surgery Sue Doll"* once, but later call it, *the doll, your model, Sue,* or even *your product.* You've warmed up your speech and connected by using a product name, but you haven't overused it to the point of distraction.

CONNECT BY USING THE WORDS OF YOUR AUDIENCE

Anytime you can refer back to something said by a participant during the session, you will help to connect further with your group. *"When George asked me that question earlier today about bringing costs down, I was struck by how much budgets are influencing our medical units at this time."* You've used a participant's name, paid him the compliment of remembering his words, and now bridged his obviously important question into the next part of your speech. *"During the meeting today, Scott and Ted have both raised questions about finances. Let's turn our attention in that direction now...."* Again, you've used their names, observed and remembered their comments, and strongly indicated you are taking the presentation in the direction of their interests. Who wouldn't feel complimented by such attention from a speaker?

We all like to hear our own names; we like to hear the names of our products and other familiar aspects of our business and our lives. If you can't use a proper noun to create an inclusive feeling, use one of the five personal pronouns or their derivatives. And with each choice, consider its ability to help you connect with your listener. Words have the power to help us connect.

SUMMARY: USE WORDS TO CONNECT

- Use personal pronouns.
- Use participants' names.
- Use synonyms to refer to similar content without sounding like a stuck record.
- Use words and labels participants use.
- Refer to participants' words and phrases later in your speech.

Notes

[1] John F. Kennedy, inauguration address, January 20, 1961.

[2] Winston Churchill, address to the British House of Commons on Dunkirk, June 4, 1940.

[3] Armstrong, BC, Canada – the city is named Armstrong and the surrounding Municipality is Spallumcheen. Historically, both entities are recognized equally thus local societies often bear the name of both.

CHAPTER 10

USE VISUAL AIDS TO CONNECT

Endless overhead slides or a repetitive on-line presentation[1] do not serve to connect speakers to their audiences. In fact, visual aids often isolate the speaker from the listener and are frequently chosen as a sort of a crutch. Many speakers tell me they use visual aids so they don't have to go to the trouble of learning their whole speech. They transfer almost every sentence to a slide and virtually read it to the audience. Many of these misguided speakers darken the room for an on-line presentation, thus further distancing themselves from the audience. You've likely been present in the audience for such a session, so you know the speaker wasn't using the visual aid to connect with you.

VISUAL AIDS HAVE MANY PURPOSES

Visual aids have many legitimate purposes beyond connecting with the audience, but they should at least do no harm to the speaker-audience relationship. Visuals are exceptional tools for illustrating difficult concepts and providing statistical information in easily interpreted graphic form. They can be used to add variety to some portion of a presentation or, as noted in the chapter on humour, give the audience a chance to laugh. Visuals can be used to offer information such as the title, author, and publisher for a book when the speaker quotes from it. Of course this information can also be offered in handout material which is itself a form of visual aid. These legitimate uses of visual aids help to illustrate and add variety, but do not necessarily serve to connect the speaker to the audience.

VISUALS CAN CONNECT YOU TO YOUR AUDIENCE

However, visuals can offer another way to improve the relationship between speaker and audience. When a visual is carefully chosen and well handled, it can involve the audience. You have many visual tools to choose from and need only use them creatively to make sure they have their desired effect. Your choices include objects, flats,[2] models,[3] and projected visuals such as overhead slides, on-line presentations, 35mm slides, video clips and printed handout material. Even costume or special staging effects could be used as visual aids. The following examples will help you see how a creative approach to using visuals can connect you to your audience.

Judy,[4] a student in one of my public speaking classes and an avid biker, spoke about the need for motorcycle helmets. She began by dropping an egg onto a prepared surface. As you'd expect, the egg smashed open and egg innards spilled over the waiting absorbent paper. Judy told us this would also happen to a human brain when its owner flew off the motorbike in an accident – unless that human brain was protected by a helmet.

After an informative speech about selecting the right helmet, Judy concluded her speech with another egg demonstration. She laid fresh paper on her table top, used additional paper toweling to fashion a little helmet for the egg, secured the helmet with a generous coating of masking tape, and held the egg high above the table for its test flight. It landed, bounced and rolled, but didn't appear to break. Judy used a small knife to open the helmet for a closer inspection of the egg, and sure enough, it appeared in good condition. She used this object lesson, which held us spellbound, to confirm her message that helmets save lives.

Judy used simple household items and a little mystery to connect with us. Her message and her demeanor were serious, yet the audience was intrigued and entertained. Her movements were controlled and efficient in both demonstrations, leaving her ample time to pause as she held the egg prior to freefall, to make eye contact and gauge our readiness for the event, and to let us react to the egg's impact. The visual itself, the creative way it was incorporated, and Judy's delivery were all important in making sure the demonstrations connected her to her audience.

Another speaker, Terri,[5] in motivating others to use public speaking as a tool for personal success, spoke of her own evolution from reluctance to eloquence in only a few months. She told us she had a list of fears from March of the previous year and asked if we'd like to know what was on it. The audience quickly begged to see the list. She removed a blank sheet on her flip chart to reveal a neatly printed list.

Fear of being eaten by a grizzly bear topped her list, then fear of public speaking, fear of dying in an earthquake, fear of public speaking, fear of a gas explosion, fear of public speaking, and so on. We quickly saw the humour, and after giving us time to laugh, she covered the list and moved away from her flipchart to signal a transition in her speech. This use of the flipchart was creative and achieved its goal in mere seconds. The speaker let us laugh at her, she made her point in only a few words, and once she had our attention and interest was able to shift easily back to her inspirational message.

CREATIVE USE OF PROJECTED VISUALS CONNECTS

Projected visuals have become very popular in boardroom presentations, seminars, and meetings. The traditional slide with five lines of text, each limited to five words, is superb for reinforcing your message and serves as a subtle crutch to help you stay focused and on schedule. To use the projected visuals to connect, you'll need to seek creative approaches such as the one described below.

I once saw a speaker use an overhead projector to display four silhouettes of common shapes: a square, a triangle, a circle, and a hexagon (Figure 1). She asked us to select the shape we thought best described our personality. On a second slide the four shapes appeared again, each in a quadrant (Figure 2) created by the intersection of a vertical and horizontal axis. She explained that one shape, perhaps the circle, would be chosen by those of us who had strong people skills and would succeed at careers involving selling and motivating others. The square was for analytical types, the triangle for relaters, and the hexagon for entrepreneurs and other leaders. Our speaker claimed her two-minute exercise was as accurate as any detailed personality profile. I'm not sure we all believed her but we had fun.

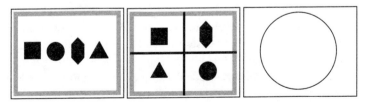

Figure 1: Choose a shape that best represents your personality.

Figure 2: Those of you who chose the circle are...

Figure 3: Transparent circle is laid over Figure 2 (onlay technique) as the final step.

I later edited this the activity for regular use in a motivational seminar for young adults. The theme of their conference revolves around volunteer leadership and creative contributions to their community. I use a similar opening slide (Figure 1) and ask the audience to pick the one that best describes their personality. But when I show them the shapes in the quadrant (Figure 2), I ask them to identify themselves with the figure. *"Who chose this one?"* I say, referring to the circle. A few participants raise their hands, and I tell them they are the creative ones in the room. They usually seem very pleased with this assessment while the others impatiently await their designation. The next shape I attribute to the leaders, *"In this group we have everyone from Mother Teresa to Attila the Hun."* When we reach the last group, most of the stragglers identify themselves. I reveal their true identity, *"Lives completely concerned with sex and booze,"* to peals of laughter. These are college-aged adults, and even if they aren't indulging in alcohol or sexual intimacies, they see the humour in this depiction of a party animal.

There is a final part to this simple visual routine, for although the second slide connects through humour, I want the slides to connect my audience to the points I've made in my speech. I use an overlay or onlay technique[6] with a transparent circle (Figure 3) on the top slide. I explain that in reality we all need to use all of the skills. I place the circle towards the lower right quadrant and explain there are times when creativity is essential. I shift the circle to the quadrant above and remind them there are times when they'll need to show leadership. When I reach the last quadrant I say, *"And there are times when you just need to party — to kick back, relax, and reflect on all you've accomplished."* From there I am ready to move into my closing, and they are connected and ready to hear my final message.

CONNECTING WITH VISUALS DEPENDS ON A DELIBERATE DELIVERY

When I took my teacher's training in the early 1970's, we were given a full day's training on the use of audiovisual aids. There weren't nearly the choices there are today and many were unsophisticated. Most overhead slides made in schools were made on a thermofax machine. Our instructor called it a "tie-ironer." After he'd referred to it several times, one of my colleagues asked the question our instructor had obviously been expecting, the answer to which we all wanted to know, *"Why are you calling it a tie-ironer?"* Without skipping a beat, our instructor removed his tie, showed us it was somewhat wrinkled from being knotted at his neck, and then fed it into the rollers of the thermofax unit. It slipped out the other side neatly pressed. This gave him an opportunity to explain the simple workings of the unit which used heat and a roller system to create transparencies. He'd connected with his student-teacher audience by using a simple demonstration, a small amount of anticipation, some audience participation, showmanship, and humour. Twenty-something years later, at least one of his students still remembers the moment and the point he made.

CAUTION! BAD IDEA AHEAD

An extremely well-known platform motivator addressing a luncheon crowd of nearly 2000 wore a light-coloured shirt with a vest under it. As he spoke about giving more than 100% effort to achieving your goals, he appeared to perspire profusely, as if he was giving more than 100% to his motivational message. Some people in the audience thought he was sweating, and I suppose that's what he wanted us to think, but the wetness was in a peculiar pattern that exactly matched the vest under his shirt, rather than the normal places where sweat appears. As he spoke he frequently beat his hands against his chest and upper abdomen to give emphasis to his message of effort and reward. With each contact, moisture flew through the air onto the front rows of the group. Several got up and left in disgust, some stayed but shielded themselves each time he thumped and sprayed, while others seemed unaware or simply seemed to accept this as the price you pay to be close to your guru.

Although he is generally regarded as one of the most successful motivational speakers on the circuit, his performance lost him a lot of supporters that day. Nearly half of the evaluations rated it as poor. Although he made some other mistakes that might have contributed to their response (including going overtime), I think the audience was, at least in part, responding to a poorly crafted visual aid, a sweat vest that doused those sitting closest to the speaker.

COSTUMES AND STAGE EFFECTS CAN CONNECT

Costumes and stage effects are often used in motivational platform speaking, and in many cases they do help transport the audience to an accepting state of mind. Morgan MacArthur,[7] winner of the 1994 World Championship of Public Speaking, often uses costuming to alter the mood of his audience. Morgan has expressive black eyebrows and a massive black handlebar mustache. A veterinarian from Idaho, he wears an enormous black ten-gallon hat and authentic cowboy boots.

The costume helps him establish his favourite persona, sort of a simple country lad with a few bits of folk wisdom to share. His audiences adore him for his humility and folksy suggestions; the costuming helps him visually reinforce this image and connect with his audience.

INVOLVE THE AUDIENCE WITH YOUR VISUALS... YOU'LL CONNECT

I've often seen speakers involve the audience while working with flat visuals. Let's assume you need to show your award-winning photograph of the inside of a shark's mouth. You've had it enlarged to poster size and mounted on foamcore to make it rigid. You could pre-arrange assistance from an early arrival seated near the front, you could ask for volunteers, or you could select someone and ask if he or she would mind helping by holding your shark. You can also use volunteers or conscriptees to write on your flip charts and whiteboards or blackboards. Reassure them that spelling doesn't count and thank them sincerely when they finish. Volunteers can assist you with other visuals such as holding your model or prop, temporarily donning a costume item, adjusting the lighting levels in the meeting area, or standing guard over a fragile model following your speech.

ANOTHER WORD OF CAUTION!

Avoid audience participation where the interaction with the visual is demeaning. At the opening of a major conference, the keynote speaker asked for six volunteers. They readily leapt into the spotlight and he gave each a hat. One had a beanie topped with a propeller, another had a construction hard hat, a third had a flower-laden garden bonnet and so on. He proceeded to label three of his volunteers with a set of negative characteristics and used them in a poorly crafted role-play. One of his volunteers liked the stage and frequently upstaged him with her remarks, and another was either so dense or so terrified of the stage he couldn't perform the simplest requests. Our speaker never did identify the other three personalities, so we had no idea why they were at the front wearing the ridiculous hats.

As I sat in the audience, I felt embarrassed for his volunteers. The woman seated next to me was mystified by his performance and asked if I knew what this activity was about. The man seated on the other side said he was sure he'd seen our speaker use it before but in another speech, and he thought maybe he was still experimenting with the technique. Like many others in the audience, my seat mates were engaging in dialogue. The visuals were intriguing, he'd engaged volunteers, but since he hadn't connected the performance to his message, his audience had disconnected.

MAKE IT MEANINGFUL TO CONNECT

Each time you involve your audience in a meaningful way in your visual presentation, you have another opportunity to connect with them. Those who volunteer are usually happy to help you and to play a minor role in your presentation. They are often the first to ask questions and visit you following your presentation to thank you for your excellent speech.

You can see from the examples, both good and bad, how important delivery skills are in working with visuals. Careful preparation and rehearsal, allow you to move smoothly into and through your visual performance while making eye contact to gauge awareness and add intensity to the performance. Without adequate planning and preparation, your attention is on the visual itself rather than on your audience, and your chances of connecting are at best slim.

SUMMARY: USE VISUAL AIDS TO CONNECT

- Keep your visuals simple.
- Select your visuals with your audience in mind and set them up so everyone can easily see them.
- Whenever possible, work with full lighting so you can easily be seen.
- Focus on your audience rather than your visual.
- Involve your audience if possible – but not if it will embarrass anyone.
- Help your audience make the connection between your visual and your content.

Notes

[1] *"On-line presentation"* refers to slide presentations where the slide is generated in your computer and projected, through a video system (the preferred method) or alternately, through an LCD projection panel placed over the stage of the overhead projector.

2 *"Flats"* refers to all two dimensional, non-projected materials including flip charts, whiteboards, blackboards, pin boards, and mounted flat material such as a map on foamcore.

3 *"Models"* refers to all three dimensional, non-projected visuals such as scientific and architectural models.

4 Judy Johnson, Johnson Hall and Associates.

5 Terri L. Dickneider, Toastmasters of the Desert, January 13, 1998.

6 *"Overlay or onlay technique"* refers to superimposing one slide or image on another. In a traditional overhead presentation this is done by laying one transparency over another. In an on-line presentation, such as PowerPoint or WP Presentation, or a 35mm slide show, this effect is achieved with multiple slides or builds.

7 Morgan MacArthur currently lives in New Zealand where he sells veterinary pharmaceuticals and speaks professionally. In 1994 he won the World Championship of Public Speaking.

SECTION FOUR: STRATEGIES FOR CONNECTING

CHAPTER 11

THE RIGHT SET-UP HELPS YOU CONNECT

ONE OF YOUR FIRST DELIVERY CONSIDERATIONS IS THE SET-UP OF THE speaking area. This includes the room you speak in, the staging area, the set-up of chairs and tables for participants, speaker furnishings such as projection tables and a lectern, audiovisual aids, and refreshment areas. Many speakers tell me they would have been much better if the set-up were different. I always encourage them to ask for the set-up they prefer and then make adjustments if their preference isn't possible.

I like to speak with only a low table for my projector or materials when teaching and offering training seminars because I don't want a lectern to restrict my movement, but I do need somewhere for my speaking materials and visual aids. For a keynote address I prefer an open floor or stage area and a remote microphone. Again, I want to be open to my audience and not restricted by a microphone cord. If the setting is a boardroom, I'll usually choose a spot furthest from the door because this minimizes interruptions if someone arrives late or has to leave during my speech. Each choice I make is based on my speaking style, the facility available, and my audience.

ASK FOR THE RIGHT ROOM

Although the exact type of room you want isn't always available, I encourage speakers to ask for the room and set-up they need. At a conference, hotel, school or office facility you might be asked what type of room you want and your choices could include:

Boardrooms

Boardrooms work well for small audiences because they bring participants close together with the comfort of one large fixed table, or occasionally an open horseshoe or hollow square in the middle of a fairly long, narrow room. Chairs are usually comfortable, and because of the acoustics, your voice will project easily. Boardrooms are rarely attached to another meeting space, so you are unlikely to be interrupted. You'll usually have good control of lighting because windows will have drapes and the artificial light can be readily adjusted.

Projected visuals are frequently a problem because the screen must sit at one end of the room which means that your projector, and computer if required, usually have to rest between you and your audience. Those seated nearest to you, therefore, will be facing into this equipment. You might be able to arrange a lower table placed at the end of the boardroom table, or you can encourage those nearest you to push back from the table slightly.

Function or Meeting Rooms

Function or meeting rooms have moveable chairs, and the option of re-arranging tables for participants which gives plenty of flexibility to your set-up. They also have a normal ceiling height, some fabric to muffle sound, and reasonable acoustics. Projected visuals can be difficult to see if the room is large, in which case you should request a riser. Risers vary, but they usually give you eight to twelve inches of elevation, which is enough to help you hold the attention of those at the back of the room. It's tough to connect with an audience if they can't see you. Also consider the set-up of your visuals in relationship to the seating, as covered in the tips section that follows.

Ballrooms

In ballrooms you usually speak from a stage, and the seating isn't fixed. Like meeting rooms, ballrooms usually have good acoustics, proper sound systems, and frequently a technician to assist you in fine tuning. Unless you are the only speaker using the ballroom, you'll likely get a generic set-up with rows of chairs in sections divided by aisles. Suggestions of how to have the seating arranged for better audience connection can be found later in this chapter (see: Seating/Furniture Arrangements).

Policy Rooms

You speak from the bottom of a policy room, and your audience is seated behind desks on a series of risers. The risers usually curve slightly so they can look across the space at each other and you can see everyone. Your visuals will also be seen easily. This set-up is good for most kinds of informative speaking, and unless it's very crowded, your participants can readily interact with each other. Furnishings are usually fixed in policy rooms, so you won't have a lot of options beyond the designer's original layout.

Theaters

Theaters usually have curved rows of fixed seating with minimal room for movement. You might be speaking from a stage or in a pit at the bottom of the theater. Your visuals will be seen readily, but interaction will be difficult because acoustically most theaters are designed for good sound transmission in only one direction, from the speaker to the audience. If you need your audience to get out of their seats and interact, beg to be given a different facility. If you are relying heavily on projected visuals or will have an audience seated for a long time, a theater is ideal.

Auditoriums

Auditoriums usually have removable or folding seating which is frequently very uncomfortable for the audience. In schools, children are often asked to sit on the floor while you speak. In either case, you can assume your audience won't be entirely comfortable and there will be a lot of fidgeting. Auditoriums often have dreadful acoustics because they are large spaces with high ceilings, few irregular surfaces, and little fabric to soften echoes. If you must work in an auditorium, speak with your back close to a wall and invite your audience to sit near you rather than scattered throughout the space.

Classrooms

Classrooms vary but often feature individual seats with writing surfaces attached or tables for two or more learners. It's rare to find one set for more than forty or fifty participants, so acoustics are good, visuals can be seen, and you won't need a riser or platform to be seen. Other than being plain and utilitarian, classrooms are usually adequate places to speak.

Restaurants and Dining Rooms

Dining areas are frequently all that's available if you are delivering a breakfast, lunch, or dinner speech. With a small group in a pleasant, bright facility, this rarely poses a problem, but with a larger group it can be tricky. You'll need to arrange for a sound system because few restaurants are designed for speakers and the best are designed to reduce noise transmission from one table to the next. When selecting an area in which to speak, pay attention to obstructions such as pillars and beams, and watch for lighting which can be dazzling because of windows or far too dim if the restaurant is cavelike. Avoid relying on visual aids when speaking in restaurants.

Lounges

Lounge areas in hotels and restaurants are sometimes used for late afternoon functions. If you are unfortunate enough to have to speak in this setting, at least try to ensure the guests will have seating where they can easily face you. Acoustics are usually dreadful, lighting is dim at best, there's rarely a sound system, and interference from the usual activities of a lounge are almost a certainty. Furthermore, unless the facility has just been built, a distinctive odor will permeate everything. After several engagements of this type, my strongest recommendation borrows from the U.S. drug education campaign, *"Just say 'NO'."*

Outdoor Venues

Outdoor spaces are infrequently used as the main facility for a speaker but they are sometimes offered as breakout space for a program. When speaking outdoors improve the acoustics by keeping your back against something solid such as a wall or a large rock, speak facing the sun so your audience can see you without being blinded, and don't use visuals that need power.

If you are using an outdoor area for breakout activities, use a whistle or gong to signal participants when you need their attention. If the outdoor space is undefined and participants could stray quite a distance, pre-set time limits can be helpful, *"According to my watch it's 9:15. This exercise will take about ten minutes. Let's agree to return by 9:25,"* or you can purchase an airhorn[1] as a signal to return.

Private Offices

Private offices are occasionally used for business presentations. Since these are small, you might want to stay seated during your presentation to avoid towering above your audience. Acoustics won't be a problem and lighting is usually adjustable, but using visuals will require some adjustment. I've seen speakers present on-line using the computer screen, which works fine, if you only have a few participants.

TIPS ON ADJUSTING YOUR TOOLS SO YOU CAN CONNECT

If you don't ask, you certainly won't get what you need, but even if you get exactly what you asked for, most speakers find they still need to make some adjustments when they arrive at the speaking site. No matter what you ask for, some facilities will ignore their promises and some simply won't be able to comply. Again, your job is to make choices that make it easiest for the audience to stay attentive and interested. The following tips will help you make an informed decision.

LIGHTING

Avoid speaking with your back to windows or any other bright light source.[2] The bright light behind you makes your face appear deeply shadowed and your audience will find it difficult to look into the light. Even on a dull day, try to speak where the windows are to one side of you, or if you must, look into the bright light yourself. You'll find it difficult to see your audience, but at least they'll be blissfully unaware of your problem and completely focused on you.

Take time to learn about the artificial lighting in your meeting space. How is it adjusted? Can you handle the lights or will you need a volunteer? Asking an audience member to assist you with the lighting provides an opportunity to personally connect with them and most folks are happy to help.

Unless your speech begs for low mood lighting, which is sometimes the case in dramatic or interpretive speeches, use as much light as you can without destroying the visibility of your projected visuals. Light tends to make us feel energetic, which is good for both listeners and speakers. Whatever lighting you choose, try to keep your face in the light, so your audience can focus on the source of the speech and a strong visual connection with you is made possible.

In programs lasting several hours, you can refresh the audience periodically by altering the level of the lighting. However, I've seen several speakers finish a segment where they had the lights low for projection purposes, and then suddenly turned on the brightest lights in the room. This was startling and unpleasant for their audiences. Far better to adjust the light level gradually or at least warn the audience they are about to be illuminated.

If speaking in a theater, you might find stage lights glaring up into your face, a spotlight following you, and a darkened house. Ask to have the house lights on and reduce the strength of the lights on you so that you can see your audience. Most theaters have the capacity to adjust lighting, and it's worth the effort to request exactly what you need.

SOUND / NOISE

Unless you like to hear cheering and laughter from the room next door, avoid meeting rooms where a folding wall separates you from the stand-up comic in the adjacent room. If you are a noisy speaker, or frequently cause your audience to be noisy, warn the facility of the complaints they'll receive if you aren't placed away from other speakers. I'm amazed how often a better room is suddenly available.

External sound from trains, planes, ambulances, or any other nearby noises can also undermine your brilliant delivery. You can't always eliminate them but you can find ways to adjust. When I spoke in a building situated beside the main runway of an international airport, the departure of each jumbo jet was impossible to ignore. By arrangement with the group, every time a jet was too noisy we'd all take a quick stretch break. To give me a break, I asked participants to take turns leading the stretch. A model plane was passed to the new leader as soon as the roar began as a signal to start our stretch break.

Try to eliminate noise within the building too. The hum of an exuberant air conditioning unit or the sputtering of overhead lighting can usually be handled with a call to maintenance. When the hotel I was speaking in at Whistler, British Columbia, a ski resort village, decided to completely remodel but neglected to tell the host group of their plans, we arrived to find open ceilings with the continuous pounding of air hammers and the shriek of drills. Threats worked to rectify the annoyance. When told the bill would not be paid and a general announcement suggesting boycott would go out to various business and professional associations in Canada, the crew amazingly found quieter activities to keep them busy.

Seating / Furniture arrangements

Seating arrangements are another important consideration. Theater seating (Figures 4, 5, 10 and 11) brings your audience closer to you but doesn't encourage interaction or note-taking, while classroom seating (Figures 6 and 7) is well suited to seminars or meetings where you want the group to write or have some interaction with each other.

Whether you select classroom or theater venues, most hotels provide a very basic layout (Figures 4 and 6), but you can often give the room a more spacious feel and increase visibility both for the speaker and the audience by curving the seating slightly (Figures 5 and 7). Audiences seem to interact with each other better when they can see each other. Also, when one person asks a question, the others are more attentive because they are getting a visual image along with the verbal input.

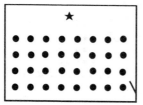

Figure 4: Typically a hotel will set chairs in straight rows for a theatre type arrangement. Figure 5 is often better.

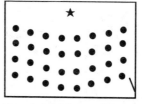

Figure 5: A slightly curved formation improves everyone's visibility and seats an equal number of participants, but you'll need to sketch it for most facilities or rearrange the chairs yourself.

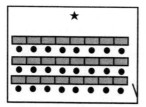

Figure 6: Typical classroom set-up with small tables for two or three. Figure 7 is often better.

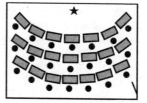

Figure 7: Again, curving the tables slightly give a more spacious feel and better visibility for speakers and listeners.

If your goal is participation and the group is small, consider a horseshoe (Figure 8) or boardroom setting (Figure 9). Both bring groups into a closer range, but as noted earlier, the boardroom setting causes some difficulties for projecting visuals.

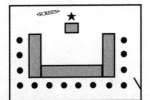

Figure 8: Horseshoe set-up is excellent for participation. Note the projection screen can be placed slightly to one side.

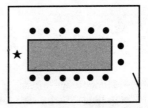

Figure 9: Boardroom set-up suits very small audiences where interaction is desirable.

In a large ballroom or convention hall, seating is frequently curved slightly but a center aisle, no matter where the doors are, is a common set-up (Figure 10). If you are one of those speakers who feels you must move out into your audience,[3] you'll need this aisle. Otherwise, ask for side aisles (Figure 11) so the bulk of your audience is in front of you instead of wasting prime territory.

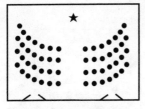

Figure 10: Typically a center aisle is provided so a big empty space is right in front of the speaker. Figure 11 is often better.

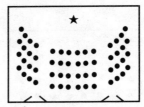

Figure 11: Creating two slightly smaller aisles to the sides puts more of the audience right in front of the speaker and facilitates participant movement.

If you have a larger space and are delivering a workshop, you might choose tables in rounds (Figure 12) or a chevron (Figure 13). Participants face you but can easily move into small discussion groups. If you are speaking at a banquet, rounds are most common, but with eight or ten at a table, some participants will have their backs to you. Manage this situation by encouraging your audience to rotate their chairs or move their chairs to a more comfortable position.

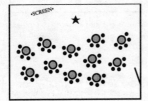

Figure 12: For participation in large groups request round banquet tables.

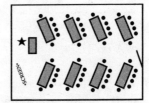

Figure 13: The chevron is an alternative way to group larger audiences for participation.

Equipment set-up

Projection Screens

In a huge ballroom or theater, your projection screen is often enormous and not moveable. Since you'll be speaking from a stage or risers, both you and your visuals (assuming they are of suitable quality) will be easily viewed. When a screen isn't fixed, you can improve visibility by ordering a large, free-standing screen which you place on a slight diagonal off to one side of the room (Figure 8, 12 and 13). Keep your image high on the screen rather than filling it right to the bottom where only those seated at the front will be able to view it.

Projectors

Projection equipment varies greatly in quality and ease of use. Ask for what you need, learn what is available,[4] and determine your best option. In large convention-oriented facilities, a professional audio-visual firm usually equips meetings and conferences. Most will do everything in their power to make your presentation work. In most smaller facilities and less formal situations, you'll have to arrange the equipment and its set-up yourself.

If you do a lot of speaking and have a strong preference for a certain type of projector, invest in one you like and take it with you. My overhead projector has been travelling with me for more than fifteen years. It's had one bulb burn out and a minor cord repair, but otherwise has faithfully projected many times each month for less than a hundred dollars a year. I take my own laptop if I'm using on-line presentations, and I carry my own extension cords. You don't want the audience worrying whether or not you can manage your visuals. Bringing your own equipment ensures your peace of mind and makes your use of visuals as seamless as possible.

Pointers

If you need a pointer, consider the size of the room and audience before making your choice. Your hand or a simple extension pointer are fine for small audiences. On a traditional overhead you can use a pen. You lay it on the stage of the projector so it touches the area where you want audience focus. You can use a laser pointer when your screen is large. With on-line presentations you can also use the mouse, your keypad, or even a remote mouse to have the cursor serve as a pointer.

Whichever system you use, hold it still while you indicate where you want your audience to look. Although you needn't become a slave to any system, try this pattern to help your audience stay with you: point, pause to look at your audience, and then speak about the area you've indicated.

Lecterns and Podiums

If you need to prop up your notes, ask for a lectern.[5] The most flexible type sits on a table, so you can easily push it into a comfortable position where you can maintain eye contact and be visible to your audience. If the lectern is a hefty free-standing model (it often is in hotels and convention centers), make sure you can be seen from behind it or ask that a podium or riser be placed behind it to elevate you slightly. If the lectern can be dismembered, remove the top and set it on a table. If this isn't an option, turn your lectern at a slight angle, with the side closest to the center of your audience angled about 45 degrees towards them. Your notes can still rest on the lectern, but you'll be visible to most of your audience, definitely a plus if you want to stand a chance of connecting with them.

Easels and Flip Chart Stands

If you need a flip chart, insist on one with a solid back, and if you need paper and pens, order them too. An inexpensive chart stand will often have three legs, a bar along the top to hold your paper, and nowhere to set pens. Writing on this flimsy rig produces poor results and will interfere with your presentation going smoothly. Your audience will be distracted by your struggle to deal with this thing instead of connecting with you and your message.

Most chart stands will hold mounted flat material or you can improvise by placing a chair on a table. Your visual, assuming it is mounted on rigid material, can rest on the seat and recline slightly against its back with the table giving plenty of elevation. Depending on your style and the audience, you can even involve participants by having them hold your flat visuals briefly.

Objects, Models, and Samples

Suppose you've got a food model of five pounds of ugly fat or you want to unveil your company's latest soft drink invention. These are fascinating objects that would distract many listeners from your initial message. You can arrange some sort of screening so the audience doesn't see your visual immediately. Most facilities will have cloth-covered screening units or can at least supply extra tablecloths for draping.

The bright blue plastic princess phone mentioned previously, which was used to breathe life into a customer service proposal, was stashed in the speaker's briefcase. A cellular phone appeared to ring, the speaker interrupted herself to open her briefcase and take a call, but instead of her cell phone drew out the amusing children's toy and immediately launched into a call. Having that toy on display from the start of her speech could have undermined her executive image, so her careful planning was vital in making this slightly risky move a seamless part of her presentation.

Sound systems

If your audience can't hear you they won't be attentive, and you can't connect with an audience that won't listen. If you need a microphone, use one rather than making your audience strain to hear you or straining your voice in an effort to be heard.

Hands-free Microphone

If you like to move freely as you speak, arrange for a remote lapel-type microphone. You'll need a belt or firm waistband for the battery pack, and the tiny microphone will clip onto your shirt, blouse, tie, or jacket. Work with a technician or volunteer to adjust the sound level and determine the best position for your microphone. While testing the microphone, move to all areas of the room where you will speak to determine if any loudspeakers will create a feedback[6] problem. When not speaking to your audience, turn your system off using the switch on the battery pack. This habit prevents the embarrassment of projecting a private conversation into a meeting room.

Cord-free Microphone

If you prefer, you could request a remote hand-held microphone. This is an excellent choice if you wish to involve participants and will need to amplify their responses. When not using this microphone, turn it off or lay it down gently on a padded surface so you won't amplify the contact noise. Have one location where you set your microphone so you can easily locate it later. Without a cord to identify its whereabouts, this microphone tends to vanish without a trace.

Lollipop on a Cord

The most common microphone is hand-held with a cord attached. This allows you some movement, permits you to amplify participant responses, and tends to be quite reliable. Hold it four to six inches below your mouth so air from words containing the letters *p* and *f* passes over the top; otherwise, the air creates a rustling noise.

Tethered Microphones

You can also order a lapel or lavaliere[7] microphone with a cord, but they usually feel heavy because of the cord dragging behind. For many speakers the result is disruptive because they constantly need to move and adjust the cord. It's like being tethered.

Adjusting the Corded Microphone

If you order a lectern it will likely have a microphone attached. The microphone is usually on a gooseneck stand so you can readily adjust it to a position below your mouth, but if you are like many speakers, you'll find yourself leaning over the lectern to talk into the microphone. To prevent this, ask for additional microphone cord, and then unclip the microphone at its base and lift it off the lectern. The short cord was probably attached through a hole in the top of the lectern, so you can just let it lie there. Attach the longer cord to the microphone, but do not route it through the lectern. It might not appear quite as tidy, but now you'll have a standard hand-held microphone that allows freedom of movement, better posture because you aren't leaning over the lectern, and better sound because you can position the microphone below your mouth. If you need both hands free, you can set the microphone back on the lectern. A simple change of cords gives you amazing control and flexibility.

Sharing a Microphone

If you are sharing a fixed microphone with others, you'll need to adjust it to your preferences before they speak, and likely readjust it as you begin your presentation. Do this efficiently and set it right before you begin your remarks. If you've seen a tall speaker hunched over a microphone set too low or a diminutive speaker on tiptoe, desperately stretching towards a microphone, you know how important it is to get it right. Your voice is better, and the audience can more comfortably watch you when your posture and chin position look relaxed and normal.

Avoiding Sound System Feedback

If you do get the loud squealing and squawking of feedback, immediately stop talking and lower, or move away from your microphone.

Loudspeakers located in the ceiling or behind you on a stage are most likely to be a problem. Move away from them or reduce the sound level on the system. Try speaking again but don't continue your speech until the sound has been adjusted properly. Your audience will appreciate your efforts to make them comfortable.

REFRESHMENTS

Your voice will perform better and with less strain if you have water. Pause periodically to sip and swallow. If the facility can't provide it, bring your own supply with you. I have met speakers who always bring their own water in preference to local water, believing their bodies are better used to it. If you have an unpredictable digestive system or like the comfort of drinking your favourite water, definitely haul it along.

Participants should also have a source of water available in the meeting room. It can be placed on tables if they are provided or set to one side if seating is theater style.

Talking while others eat is rarely pleasant and often seems like a waste of good words, but if you're short of time, talking during a meal might be the only option. Suggest closed sandwiches served buffet or family style for the least disruption. Avoid wrapped foods such as candy bars or packages of crackers. The disruption of plastic being ripped off food items has caused despair in more than one speaker.

Large meals tend to make participants sleepy, so if you're going to be with the group for a full day, consider having a light lunch served and a fruit or sweet plate delivered during an afternoon break. Small meals are easier for you to manage while working, and most participants seem to prefer several light food breaks rather than one enormous meal.

If you are speaking for more than three hours, do try to eat and drink periodically.[8] Your brain will function better and you'll find you have far more energy. Fruit such as bananas, grapes, raisins, and apples are easy to eat, provide moisture and nutrients, are low in fat, and rarely have adverse side effects. If you are speaking in an area where sanitation is a concern, eat only fruit you peel yourself (oranges and bananas are good choices) to prevent a sudden date with the porcelain throne.

Summary: The right set-up helps you connect

- Ask for a suitable meeting space and helpful furnishings. Explain the benefits to the organizing or hosting group and the meeting facility.
- Find out what equipment is available and select wisely with your audience and meeting facility in mind.
- When you arrive, re-arrange furnishings, lighting, visual aids, and other materials until you have maximized your set-up.
- Work with the organizers to provide suitable refreshments for you and your audience.

Notes

[1] A can of air with an airhorn attachment is available at automotive supply stores. They are exceedingly loud. Outdoors this is useful, but indoors you'll need to muffle the sound by placing your hand in the bell of the horn.

[2] Another strong light source is an overhead projector left on with no slide in place. If you stand in front of the projection screen with that bright white surface glaring behind you, your audience will have a hard time watching you and staying attentive.

[3] Moving out into a large audience, a technique used by some motivational speakers, creates problems for many members of the audience. Those seated in the front rows will have to turn to even see your back. Some of them chose the front seats because they have hearing or vision loss. By sitting close to the speaker they can lip read and see more of your expressions. When you move throughout your audience you make this impossible.

[4] The options amongst projected visual aids are changing rapidly, so I've made no attempt to direct you to any one system over another. Traditional overhead projectors and transparencies still work very effectively but are rapidly being replaced by on-line visuals. Their effectiveness varies greatly because they depend on several types of technology, a creator who has some design sense, some creativity, and enough self-discipline to use only those techniques that truly improve the presentation.

[5] Also called a *podium* by many speakers. The word *podium* also means a small raised platform such as the one an orchestra leader stands on to

conduct, so if you order a podium be sure to say you want to rest your notes on it. A tiny raised platform won't be very helpful.

6 Feedback is caused when the microphone hears itself. If you are speaking close to a loudspeaker the microphone hears your voice coming from the loudspeaker as well as what you are currently saying. The resulting high-pitched squeal is called feedback.

7 The lavaliere microphone dangles from your neck rather like a pendant.

8 Alcohol-based beverages are a poor choice. They tend to dehydrate you and they also dull your senses. You might think you're doing very well and later learn your articulation was poor, you offended several people with your unplanned jokes and you left a zipper or buttons open thus exposing areas of your body you wouldn't normally display when speaking.

Some speakers find caffeine, dairy products, soda pop, or even fruit juice troublesome. Caffeine, found in coffee, tea, and colas is a diuretic so it dehydrates you, and it is a mild stimulant. Dairy products can cause thick mucus secretions for a few speakers. Soda pop can cause mild regurgitation or burping which is rarely attractive in a speaker. Fruit juices, due to their acidic composition can cause speakers to form excessive saliva. Learn what works best for you and stick with it.

CHAPTER 12

ARRIVAL — WORK IT TO CONNECT

As I BOARDED THE ELEVATOR TO GO TO THE FIFTEENTH FLOOR OF A large building, I noticed a young fellow in jogging attire rushing towards the elevator and held the door while he dashed in. He thanked me, we had a brief but pleasant discussion about fitness and then parted at our appointed floors. I was on my way to the offices of a new client where I was to deliver a two-day seminar for a dozen senior people. Thirty minutes later the participants arrived and amongst them was the jogger, now attired in a blazer and slacks. He instantly recognized me and came over to introduce himself. We laughed about our chance meeting. Later in the day we discussed networking as a business activity and he brought up our earlier elevator experience. Apparently he'd told quite a few others about meeting me and said, *"I had no idea what you'd talk about during the seminar but I knew, whatever it was, I would enjoy it."* First impressions greatly influence our perception of reality.

I wouldn't describe myself as a *morning person;* I'm not noted for being a skilled conversationalist at seven in the morning, yet I wasn't behaving out of character. It is my habit to assume I could meet a client anytime after I reach the building, and I want their first impression to be positive. I also want to do everything I can during the arrival and set-up phase to improve my chances of connecting with the audience.

From the chapter on set-up and staging, you can see how important the details are. If you arrange an optimal set-up of the room and equipment, it can help you deliver smoothly. You'll also need to arrive early to check the set-up and make adjustments. If you're working at a convention center or hotel, it pays to speak to the facilities coordinator before you arrive and to go directly to meet this person when you arrive. In most cases these people will treat you better if you treat them with dignity and respect. They, or a junior, can go to the meeting area with you and help you make adjustments.

CHECK YOUR FACILITY AND TOOLS WHEN YOU ARRIVE

Sometimes you can scout the room in advance. Allow at least thirty minutes to set up, and longer if you have extensive visual requirements. When you arrive at your meeting room, check the following items (they are listed in chronological order):

Ensure all audiovisual aids are there and do a cursory check to determine their condition. An external A/V company might have to be called to the facility, so the sooner you check this one off the better your chances of getting assistance and replacement. Ask for spare batteries for the microphone if it is a remote system.

Lighting problems or air conditioning noise, because they take time to fix, should get early attention. No one in your audience will ever know you had a fluorescent tube changed, but you'll win the attention of those who would have been distracted, and those who get headaches, from the erratic flickering of a dying tube.

Now check the layout and seating arrangements. If not to your liking, either adjust them yourself or have the facility alter them. Some of the larger convention centers forbid non-employees to move furniture, but in most facilities no one will even notice if you eliminate extra chairs, arc the furniture, or slide a screen off to one side slightly.

Test the sound system if you are using one. Have a volunteer stand in each section of the room to ensure all loudspeakers are functional and your voice is projecting adequately. You'll likely have more noise in the room when you actually speak, so you should err on the side of loudness.

Set up your visuals next and do a complete test of each system including the microphone. Learn where the controls for lighting, piped-in music, and sound system are. You can deputize others to adjust the microphone volume and the lighting, but by familiarizing yourself with these items, you can better coordinate the activities of your volunteers.

Lay out your notes and materials to ensure they are in order and ready for delivery.

If you have handout material, determine how and when you want to get it out to participants. If you plan to use the material all the way through, you might want to hand it to participants when they arrive[1] or have it on their seats or on the tables. But if you only plan to use it briefly partway through your speech, consider holding onto it for distribution at that time. With a large audience, you can speed distribution by counting hand-outs into piles for each row. If you're short of time, this task can be handled by early arrivals or hosts who frequently volunteer their services.

Take a break to use the restroom and check your grooming. If you're speaking in a large room before a sizable audience, you might think a few stray hairs on your jacket or a little spinach between your front teeth would never create a problem. But you'll be talking to individuals before and after your speech and they will notice your grooming. If you are a terrific speaker and you connect well, they'll probably forgive you for laxity in the personal grooming department, but why take a chance? You don't want to give anyone in the audience a reason to reject you before they even hear you speak.

CRUISE THE ROOM AND MEET YOUR AUDIENCE

Now that you're groomed and fully ready to speak, use any spare time to talk to early arrivals. Most speakers relax during this informal conversation, and it can also provide you with an opportunity to build enthusiasm for your speech, honour your audience with your attention or even gather a last minute example for your talk.

As you speak to others informally, before your speech, you can introduce yourself as the speaker and find out what part of your topic interests the listener. Speak enthusiastically and confidently about your speech. This is not the time to say how nervous you feel, how poorly prepared you are, or how dreadful your visuals will seem. Think of it as making your audience feel glad they chose to come and hear you speak.

Many people feel honoured to meet the speaker, so as you visit with them you'll be showing your respect and interest in your audience. If your speech is to the executive of your company and will be delivered in a boardroom, it is still respectful to move about the room shaking hands and greeting participants.

If you do nothing else, ask a few questions and listen to the answers. Sometimes a participant will give you a last minute example or a useful lead-in to a story or example you planned to use. *"Just before I started speaking today I was talking with Jon* (indicate Jon with one open hand stretched in his direction), *a member of your group from Victoria Grove, and he mentioned an experience very similar to one I had…."* If you want to borrow a story from a participant, ask if you can use it and if that person would mind being identified. Most are very cooperative, but your courteous request shows you respect them and avoids any discomfort.

You can also use this time to arrange for assistants. I often talk to those seated at the back of a meeting room and ask them to give me a visual signal[2] if they can't hear me. If I need lighting adjusted partway through my speech, I'll look for a volunteer seated near the switches. You can find the volunteers you need during this period of informal communication.

Keep an eye on the time so you'll be ready to speak on schedule. Allow enough time to attach your microphone, do one last check of your visual aids and, if you will be introduced, let that person know you are ready to begin.

ESTABLISHING THE CONNECTION WITHOUT THE LUXURY OF A WALKABOUT

There are times when you won't have the luxury of a period of set-up and socializing as outlined above, but still do your best to establish a positive feeling before you speak. I have clients who have to walk into a meeting cold, set up while the participants watch, deliver their speeches, and then leave immediately.

One such client, Clarise, owns a public relations agency. Once short-listed for a contract, she often makes a presentation as the final bid. There might be two or three other agencies competing for the contract, and the client schedules each competitor for a thirty or forty-five minute concurrent time slot. As the previous group leaves, my client's group is ushered into the room. Clarise needs to set up her computer and projector for an on-line presentation, adjust the lighting, and lay out her other materials. If you face similar circumstances, you know this is far from ideal. But there are ways to manage this situation and help yourself connect.

When possible, Clarise visits the client's facility several days ahead and checks out the meeting room to determine its suitability for her visual presentation. If it isn't suitable, she'll suggest moving to another space, a request which has, surprisingly, often been accommodated. If a better room isn't available at least she knows the limitations of the facility. Clarise always takes along at least one technical support person whose job is to do all the electronic set-up, thus freeing her to greet and visit with the client team.

When I've observed her speaking, I've been impressed by her assertiveness in these circumstances. When introduced to the group, she explains the need for a short delay for set-up and suggests participants take a moment to stretch and get coffee. She walks up to each participant, introduces herself again, and makes easy conversation. After watching her the first time, I asked how she managed to talk with them all so easily, and she shared her secret. Clarise finds out who is expected at the meeting and learns a little about each participant before she arrives. She has usually been able to get this information from her contacts at the client firm.

When the visuals are ready, she moves to the speaking area and invites the group to re-seat themselves for the show. If someone is dawdling she'll often tease them into their seats, *"C'mon, the popcorn is getting cold."* I'm amazed at her spunk and yet, without her leadership, I'm not sure they'd respond nearly as well. Clarise treats them respectfully as equals, and in so doing builds a good working relationship before the formal presentation begins.

Her decisions before arrival and during set-up are critical in her success with each client. So are yours. Your audience deserves to feel the person speaking to them knows they are present and cares about their comfort, both physical and mental. You can improve your chances of connecting during your speech by recognizing your opportunities prior to the formal presentation. Build relationships before, during, and after your performance.

SUMMARY: ARRIVAL – WORK IT TO CONNECT

- Every contact counts – you need to be ON as soon as you arrive.
- Connect with the audio visual company and facility managers.

- Test your equipment and set-up with your audience in mind.

- Use leftover time to connect with participants: meet, greet, and complete your audience analysis.

- Create a relaxed atmosphere even if you can't take time for an extensive walkabout with your audience.

Notes

1 Handing printed material to participants as they arrive gives you an early opportunity to interact with them. If you have several hundred participants this isn't practical.

2 If they can't hear me easily, I ask them to cup their hands behind their ears. If the sound is too loud I ask them to cover their ears and look horrified. Once in a while I get a signal from someone I've asked. I know I appreciate the help when I'm the speaker, and as a listener, I like the sense that I can have some input if I'm having a hard time hearing the speaker.

CHAPTER 13

MAKE YOUR OPENING
REMARKS CONNECT

WHETHER YOU'VE ARRANGED FOR OPTIMAL SPEAKING CONDITIONS OR adjusted for the equipment and facility you were given, you are now about to speak. With participants who met you before the speech, you've already begun to create a positive impression. But for those who didn't meet you earlier, or in those circumstances when informal communication wasn't possible before your speech, this is your first opportunity to create a positive impression. This topic is discussed for three possible circumstances: how to begin if someone is introducing you as they normally do at a conference, how to begin when you get only a minimal introduction as you might in a business setting, and how to begin when you get no introduction.

YOUR BEGINNING: IF IT STARTS WITH A FORMAL INTRODUCTION

In a formal presentation to a large audience, you will be introduced. If this is an important presentation, write out a brief introduction and insist it be delivered as written. Sending a complete resume of your successes rarely results in a good introduction. Sending a precise script[1] makes the job easy and the results far more effective.

Because your audience can observe you, look enthusiastic as your introduction is being delivered. When nice things are being said about your illustrious past, look pleased. When you are being praised, appear appreciative. Look at your audience and smile periodically. And, if your introducer isn't delivering a sterling performance, act as if all is well. You are already onstage even though you aren't yet speaking, and how you behave influences audience perception.

When it's time to move to the speaking position, move energetically. You'll feel better and your audience will see someone who seems pleased to be there speaking. Some speakers even like to run to the front from a position near the side or back of the audience, which is fine if it suits your topic and your style. It would be a great decision for someone motivating others to a healthy goal-oriented lifestyle, but less appropriate for a technical presentation regarding safety enhancements.

As the introduction concludes, there should be some applause to welcome you. Groups vary and some won't applaud unless they have leadership, but you can get them started by applauding the person who introduced you. *"Roni, you did a great job of that introduction. Ladies and gentlemen, please join me in conveying our thanks for getting us off to such a good start."* If you hold your hands out in front and vividly clap, they'll join in and the spell of silence will be broken. They'll know you expect a reaction from them. You've begun to connect.

YOUR BEGINNING: WITH MINIMAL INTRODUCTION

Formal introductions are common when the speaker won't be known, but in business they are rare. In a business setting you might get a hand signal to take over the meeting or a slight verbal introduction such as, *"Kate Moss is here from our pensions committee to discuss proposed changes to the plan. Kate...."* There is rarely applause and seldom much fanfare. You are expected to get down to business promptly.

If you are seated, rise with energy, move efficiently to the speaking area, and make eye contact. Establish yourself as worthy of their attention.

Depending on the mood of your speech and the temperament of the audience, you might even verbally engage one or more members as you migrate to the speaking area. This seems to work well with peers; it reduces the feeling of formality that creeps into meetings where one person stands to address the others. For example, one client service representative addressing his peers paused on the way to the front to admire his buddy's blackened eye. They'd played hockey the night before, and the injury was now sensational enough to warrant attention. The personal connection helped the speaker relax, diverted attention briefly from his speech, and re-established him as part of the group.

When you reach the speaking area, take a moment to smile and greet your audience. If you've been invited to speak by a member of the group, this is the time to acknowledge that person's support. *"Mr. Blake, I appreciate your invitation to address the executive team this morning."* Look at Mr. Blake when you thank him and use a small open-handed gesture towards him. This is friendly without being effusive.

Your beginning: With no introduction

Many speeches begin without any introduction at all of the speaker. In this case, stand confidently in the speaking position and look at the audience. If your audience doesn't immediately give you their attention, you can use a verbal cue such as *"Good morning. We're about ready to begin,"* followed by a pause and direct eye contact. Alternately you can gain their attention by flashing the room lights, illuminating a visual or making an unusual sound.[2]

If your audience knows you, you can simply greet them and begin your planned remarks. If your audience doesn't know you, take a moment to introduce yourself. Keep this brief but do let them know who you are and your main qualifications for speaking to them. If you're talking about raising children, your own family is relevant. If you're discussing the future of telecommunications technology for business, your engineering degree and research interests are more appropriate.

If you need to introduce yourself, keep the focus on your audience as much as you can. *"Because I'm going to talk about children, you'll probably want to know if I've ever had any or if I'm just one of those overly educated experts. I do have a background in child psychology but most of what I'll offer I've put to the test with my own four children, aged eight to seventeen years."* Talking about yourself has the potential to distance the speaker from the audience unless you focus each statement on their needs and interests.

You can also briefly explain your connection to an individual or group during this self-introduction. *"Your president, Charlie, invited me to be here tonight. He and I have struggled to get sponsors for our school breakfast program, so I think he knew I'd willingly talk with your group about the connection between brain development and nutrition."* If the audience is part of Charlie's group and you're one of his close associates, you're virtually a part of their group now. This closer connection makes it easier to win their interest and support.

CONNECT THROUGH CONTENT AS YOU START TO SPEAK

Too often I've seen speakers who leapt right into the technical details of their speech without proper orientation for the audience. The precise content of your opening will vary with the audience, the topic, the setting, and your style but consider including the following:

Greeting

A greeting to the audience is always appropriate. In a business speech this is exceedingly brief, *"Good morning,"* while in a more social context you might be more expansive, *"Good morning, ladies and gentlemen. I'm pleased to be here to talk with you today because... and I want to compliment you on...."*

Motivational speakers sometimes insist on audience participation here by loudly saying *good morning* with a slight rise in pitch at the end, as if asking for a response, and then waiting. They wait with eyes focused on the audience and an open-armed gesture almost as if conducting an orchestra. They expect the audience to say *good morning* in response. If the response is meager or non-existent, they'll repeat the greeting. Even dull, sleepy audiences respond by the second attempt, and the speaker already has won participation and connected with the audience.

Preview

A preview of your speech is important if you are informing or selling but less so in humorous and inspirational speeches. Look at the content of your speech; it probably has three, four, or five major parts. Simply tell the audience what those parts are and explain why you will be discussing them.

Imagine a speaker, Karim, talking to an audience of local business folk about doing environmental cleanup at Passion Creek Canyon (a mythical area). Karim might say, *"I'll begin with a brief slide show to familiarize you with our lovely Passion Creek Canyon and show you some of the environmental problems slowly creeping into this area. Then I'll describe five major areas of concern and show how each one can be improved using only a small amount of money and a moderate investment of our commitment. I'll conclude today by showing you what Passion Creek Canyon can become with a little help from all of us."* Karim has outlined the main parts of the speech and has presented them conversationally rather than as a list. You can use a visual aid to provide this outline but even if you do, you need to paraphrase in order to connect your ideas to the audience's interests.

In formal business proposals, this preview is frequently best handled by an executive summary which gives your listeners the big picture of your speech. It not only identifies the main points but also introduces your bottom line. For superb examples of executive summaries and a thorough discussion of how to use them, I recommend you read Ray Anthony's book, *Talking to the Top*.[3]

Benefit Statement

Tell your audience why they should listen to your presentation even if you think it's obvious. Again this wouldn't be needed at the start of a humorous after-dinner speech, in a toast to the bride, or a eulogy, but it is vital in speaking to inform, inspire, motivate, or sell. For example, Karim might stress how a clean Passion Creek Canyon will bring tourist dollars or notoriety to the community. Tell your audience how they'll benefit from listening to your speech.

Grabber

Grabbing your audience's attention with some type of surprise or excitement is important in most types of speaking although less so in business proposals than in more public forms of speech-making. The humorist will usually begin with a funny story or joke, the inspirational speaker could use a quotation or music, the business speaker might select startling statistics, and the instructor could tell a story. Consider a striking demonstration or surprising visual as another way to grab and win early attention. You can't connect with your audience if they aren't paying attention.

My husband's favourite university professor taught business law. He began each class with a vignette from the lives of two fictitious characters, Pat and Mike. As business partners they got into every legal difficulty imaginable and these scenarios served as memorable openings for each successive class. Some thirty-five years later he still recalls these stories and the points of law they illustrated. Now there's a professor who knew how to connect with a restless audience of undergraduates.

Housekeeping Announcements

If your presentation will be lengthy, or you have special requirements for audience participation of some type, you might choose to make some housekeeping remarks during your opening. This is where I mention I speak quickly, ask my audience to let me know if they can't hear me, tell them about the notes or materials I'll have for them later, offer to take questions all the way through my presentation, and pass on any announcements from their host group. I've been asked to tell groups where to find restrooms, smoking areas, refreshments, and resource materials. I've also been asked to announce breaks and draw for door prizes, and even to endorse the candidacy of a nominated officer. I agreed to do this last task because it was done in jest and gave me a marvellous opportunity to connect with the group.

When you do engage in housekeeping announcements, keep them succinct, clearly set them apart from the speech itself, and make every effort to ensure the group both enjoys and appreciates the messages. *"For those of you who like to indulge, smoking areas are provided outside, or indoors at the Coconut Lounge, and I have this key to your president's suite which I'll make available to the highest bidder."* Doesn't that sound more enjoyable than, *"For those of you who must smoke, go outside,"* or *"Smoking is only permitted in the lounge and outdoors."*? If you consider how it feels to your audience to hear your message, you'll soon find creative ways to give ordinary messages a touch of showmanship and pizzazz.

SHIFT INTO YOUR SPEECH CAREFULLY SO YOU DON'T LOSE THE CONNECTION

If you've offered housekeeping messages, you'll now need to switch back to the topic of your speech. Pauses before and after the transition statement help the audience adjust to the changes. At the very least you can say, *"That concludes all the housekeeping details. Now let's get down to business."* If you haven't diverted attention from the topic to the messages, you'll still need to pause after your opening to signal you are making a transition.

DELIVERY TIPS AS YOU START TO SPEAK

Your body language has an enormous impact in this opening. Imagine your audience sitting before you wondering if this will be a good use of their time. If you immediately seem enthusiastic and confident, they will begin to relax, feeling certain they've got a good speaker. Rehearse in front of a window or mirror until the image you see is a speaker with an energetic, upright posture, confident open gesture, and fluid movement.

Act "As If"

If you feel stiff or self-conscious, try acting *as if* you were a world-renowned speaker. Even though you're just acting, your audience will respond as if they had an expert in front of them.

Breathe

Take a deep breath because it will improve the quality of your voice and help you relax. Without adequate breath support, your voice won't easily project, and you'll find it difficult to sound naturally expressive. A harsh, shrill, or atonal voice won't endear you to your audience, and it can turn your mild anxiety into rampant speaking terror. The deep breath improves your voice so the first sounds you and your audience hear are those of an energetic, confident speaker. When you hear yourself sounding confident, you relax and your audience responds by relaxing too.

Smile

Subject permitting, smile at your audience. Some business speeches aren't improved by a gleeful facial expression, and a few speakers don't seem to have a genuine smile, but for most speakers, most of the time, a smile offers one more opportunity to connect. A smile is one of our earliest connections to other humans; babies are quick to associate smiles with happiness and security. Perhaps that is why, when a speaker genuinely smiles and looks at us, we connect instantly with them.

Eye Contact

Take time to look at your audience as you deliver your opening remarks. You'll notice their interest which will bolster your courage and give you an opportunity to connect on a non-verbal level. By contrast, if you are repeatedly dipping your head to refer to your notes, you won't notice your audience very much, and you certainly won't seem nearly as confident of yourself or your material.

Slow Down

Try to slow down for your opening even if you are a speed demon later on in the speech. Slowing your pace of delivery helps your audience become accustomed to your voice and gives you an opportunity to observe your audience.

Project Your Voice

Speak loudly so your voice will project as you begin. Later you can lower your voice to bring intimacy or emotion to the performance, but as you begin you want everyone to hear you easily and feel they have a leader.

Be bold in your opening. Use vivid gestures, dramatic pauses, energetic movements, an exciting tone of voice, and a little touch of drama. Take a few risks and you'll win your audience's attention, arouse their desire to hear your message, and begin to build the relationship where you connect and feel comfortable with each other. In the next chapter we'll look more closely at your delivery skills. They are a powerful tool in connecting with your audience.

SUMMARY: MAKE YOUR OPENING REMARKS CONNECT

- Write your own introduction – no one else cares as much as you do.

- While being introduced look pleased and attentive – you're already on display.

- If you introduce yourself, behave as a leader and take control.

- Help the audience by giving them only information they need to understand you and connect to you.

- Delivery counts – yours can serve to relax you and connect you to your audience.

Notes

1 I like the advice on writing introductions offered in the revised Dale Carnegie book by Dorothy Carnegie, *The Quick and Easy Way to Effective Speaking* (Simon & Schuster, New York, NY, 1962). Carnegie offers a simple T-I-S formula where T refers to topic, tell the audience what subject you'll address; I refers to Interest, tell the audience why they will be interested in this topic; and S refers to Speaker, tell the audience why the speaker (you) are qualified or appropriate to give this speech.

2 I use a wooden train whistle for small audiences and a large bell or even a small muffled air horn for larger groups. I've seen other speakers play a musical instrument such as a small xylophone or pitch pipe, and one speaker arranged for a series of indoor fireworks with light and sound that definitely got the audience's attention.

3 Anthony, Ray. *Talking to the Top.* Prentice Hall Inc., Englewood Cliffs, NJ, 1995. In addition to the useful section on executive summaries, this book is a good source of ideas for on-line presentations.

CHAPTER 14

USE YOUR DELIVERY SKILLS TO ENHANCE THE CONNECTION

SPEAKERS MUST HAVE SOMETHING OF VALUE TO SAY BUT MUST ALSO BE able to say it in a way that commands attention and wins audience support. That's why delivery is so crucial to how well you connect with your audience. Delivery skills are, in most cases, at least as important as your message because if audiences can't hear you or something about your physical performance is distracting, the best message ever crafted won't be heard.

From the examples in previous chapters, you could see that delivery skills were an integral part of the success of the techniques the speakers used. Without such basic skills as eye contact, carefully timed actions, vocal variety, and appropriate pacing, many of the techniques would distract rather than serve to connect audience, speaker, and message. First we'll look at one of those earlier examples to see how delivery skills were improved to connect the speaker to the audience. You'll see how suggestions regarding set-up and openings were incorporated as well as a general improvement in delivery skills. In the second half of this chapter, you'll get specific advice on delivery skills so you can make informed choices suited to your own presentation style, the speaking situation, and audience needs.

DELIVERY PROBLEMS WITH FIVE POUNDS OF UGLY FAT

In the chapter on humour I described the successful use a fitness instructor made of a food model; however, the first time I saw her use the five pounds of ugly fat it served only to distract her audience. She bounced up to the lectern showing the ugly yellow fat model and simultaneously asked at a rapid pace *"How many of you would like to lose five pounds of ugly fat?"* Without pausing for their response or even looking at them, she launched into all the information about her programs and how they'd help the folks lose weight. As she spoke, she fondled the fat model. Next she passed it to someone in the front row of the audience and instructed them to pass it around so everyone could fully visualize their goal. This showed a distinct lack of knowledge of her audience since quite a few of them were already slender and fit. And by passing the fat she'd lost most of their attention already. Those closest to the fat were feeling it, giggling, and chatting while others were distracted by the noise and the enticing thought of getting their turn. The fitness director rambled on and on until coffee, and then took her model and left.

That was the same speaker, the same food model, but with a total lack of delivery. She needed help not only with eye contact and timing, but also with voice, gesture, posture, staging, and movement. She'd even chosen her clothing without a thought for her audience. Her tattered track suit didn't seem a good choice for her audience which consisted mostly of professionals in tailored suits.

IMPROVING ENTRY AND STAGING

To help her connect I began with work on her entry and staging. An energetic entrance was appropriate to her presentation and her personal style, but the food model was distracting, so we agreed it could be hidden in the lectern, awaiting her arrival. This freed her hands to pin on a lapel microphone which allowed her to move more freely in the auditorium and suited her natural bouncy style. She also agreed to address the audience only after the microphone was in place, her materials were on the lectern, and she'd had time to make eye contact. This entrance, combined with a very smart-looking pantsuit, established her professionalism and won the attention of the audience.

CHANGING EYE CONTACT TO REALLY CONNECT

She believed she was making eye contact, but in fact she was gazing out at the audience without actually seeing any of them. Often called panning when a camera does this, the result is a blurred impression of the audience rather than a real connection. Gradually she became better at looking at one person's eyes and sustaining the eye contact while she finished her thought, often holding eye contact for as much as two or three seconds at a time before glancing about and focusing on another audience member.

When she needed to rely on notes, she tended to look down as she began a sentence, glance up briefly towards the middle, and quickly look down again just before she finished the point. This pattern gave her little opportunity to gauge audience response and seemed to compel her to ever greater speeds. When she looked down as she concluded her points, readying herself for the next sentence in her planned speech, she signalled the audience that the rest of the sentence wasn't very important. Once she learned to look up while she concluded her point, pause to let the audience absorb it, and simultaneously observe their reactions, she enjoyed the speaking more. She was finally realizing that her audiences wanted to hear her message.

IMPROVING VOICE

The result of these changes was apparent in how much more she noticed about the audience and how better able she was to become conversational with them. Her rapid, forced sounding voice became less rushed and more naturally expressive. By relying less on notes and memorized openings, she was also able to improve her use of posture, gesture, and movement, which in turn contributed to vocal improvement.

With the lapel microphone amplified remotely,[1] this speaker was able to move towards the audience in her opening, slip back to the lectern when she needed the food model, and then over to the coffee table to set the food model aside. Instead of clutching at her notes, the food model, or the microphone, she was able to open her hands towards the audience and use expressive and sustained gestures. When she asked how many of her audience had ever wanted to lose weight, she now stood directly in front of them and used an open, two-handed gesture which she held while awaiting their reaction. She didn't immediately get a response, so she learned to suggest a show of hands and model this when she repeated the question. This brought her an overt audience reaction. Now she was connecting and she knew it. She was having fun and a bold smile lit her face, letting the audience know they'd behaved in an appropriate manner.

STAGING PROPS AND VISUALS

After her opening remarks, she needed the food model that was behind her, tucked away in the lectern. She held up her hand as if she were a traffic officer stopping pedestrians and took five large steps back to her lectern. The audience was willing to wait because they sensed something of interest was coming. Their speaker hadn't dismissed them by turning and running away or uncomfortably skittling back to her lectern. She'd sustained eye contact throughout and kept an impish grin on her face. By hiding the model until the key moment, she staged it for maximum audience response. Now as she revealed it, the fitness director held it high and away from her body so everyone could see it simultaneously. Their gasps and giggles were her reward. She took time to enjoy their reaction before identifying the purpose of her prop and telling them they could all fondle it during the coffee break.

Now, for a change of pace, she moved to the overhead projector where she'd already placed a slide outlining the rest of the presentation. At first she read her outline to the audience, but that was boring and she lost contact with them. Her presentation improved greatly when, using her natural energy to keep it lively, she paraphrased from the list making sure she paused between points. When she reached the segment about goal setting, she indicated with an open hand the precious glob of fake fat resting beside the cookies.

Her speech slowed, she incorporated appropriate open gestures, and her eye contact and gesture were more often sustained. She began to examine the reasons for her choices. Looking at the audience gave her excellent feedback about their level of interest and attentiveness, while glancing briefly at the screen drew their attention to her visuals. Open, sustained hand-gestures felt awkward at first, but by rehearsing in front of a large window,[2] she soon saw how much better it looked than her wildly flailing hands and her favourite resting position, the figleaf.[3] She also observed that her audience relaxed once she used more open, deliberate movements and came closer to them during the opening and conclusion.

RENOVATING PHRASING

Despite all the improvements in gesture, posture, timing, and movement, this speaker was still damaging her relationship with the audience in an unusual way. After several years as a fitness instructor, she'd let her voice become overly expressive and silly at times. It probably was appropriate in the workout setting but seemed immature with this audience. Her most common problem was pitching-up[4] on statements. *"Our programs are all staffed by volunteers.",* sounded like, *"Our programs are all staffed by volunteers?"* She began to tape her remarks and play them back, and gradually learned to identify the disturbing pitch pattern. Once she was aware of it, she was able to rapidly correct the problem.

We used a similar taping / replaying / identifying approach to a second vocal problem. She often used identical phrase patterns repeatedly with a result not unlike a child repeating a nursery rhyme. At first many of her phrases were too long, and so the expression didn't match the meaning. Read the following lengthy sentence aloud and place emphasis on the underlined words to understand how she obscured her message. *"Our fitness programs rely almost entirely on volunteers like you who have some experience in the past with fitness and we'll provide some training so you can make a contribution to our programs."*

First we worked to shorten the phrases and then to place emphasis on the important words to avoid a repetitive pattern. *"Our fitness programs are usually taught by – volunteers. You could be one of those volunteers, if you have some fitness experience. Talk to me – if you'd like to volunteer. We're going to offer a fitness instructor's training course."* The goal wasn't for her to memorize or learn the speech, but rather that she become aware of the real meaning of her remarks and make sure the emphasis reflected that meaning. Once she could apply these changes to a few speech segments, her phrasing and expression also improved dramatically in normal conversation and in less formal speaking situations. By using the tape recorder as a learning tool she had become her own voice coach.

PURGING WORD CHOICES

Together we found one more excellent use for the tape recorder. Like most of us, this speaker had accumulated some favourite words, phrases, and filler noises. She often said, *"Okay – Now we're going to..."*, at the start of a sentence or *"Okay?"*, as if asking approval,[5] at the end. In the first taping we counted twenty-seven uses of the word *okay* and determined she could eliminate twenty-six of them without changing the meaning of her speech. She agreed they were excessive but argued it really wasn't that important. Once she listened to the tape of another speaker, who used many fillers and repeatedly used the word *basically*, she realized how unnecessary words and excessive *ums* and *ahs* undermine the authority of the speaker.

Excessive filler words work against a speaker because they annoy the listener. Because she wanted to build a strong relationship with her listeners, she again used the tape recorder to reduce her reliance on these meaningless and superfluous words. She would tape a small segment, play it back looking for fillers, note where they were, and try again. Using segments of under two minutes kept this exercise from becoming tedious, and she quickly learned to control her choice of language. She could have used the same technique to work on mispronunciations, grammatical errors, or poor articulation – all problems that can alienate an otherwise attentive and supportive audience.

You've just looked at one example of making choices and building delivery skills to enhance a business speech used repeatedly in company orientation sessions. In the next section, you'll find a more list-like review of the choices a speaker must make to enhance delivery when communicating to an audience. You'll again see the synergy of all the decisions you make as a speaker. For example, when you make a change in where you stand, you influence the type and amount of gesture you can use, and when you improve your posture, your voice improves.

DELIVERY SKILLS WORK IN HARMONY

Although delivery skills are broken down in this segment, they are in reality never isolated. When you work on one skill, you will usually improve many others without much effort. For example, through many years of speech coaching, I've learned to ignore filler words in the initial stages of coaching. If I mentioned them right away, they became the sole focus of many speakers. When I ignored fillers and helped speakers to make eye contact and focus on their audience, they tended to use fewer fillers anyway. If fillers were still a problem, we'd work next on their phrasing and expression. I'd help them shorten sentences and phrases and put the emphasis where it belonged. With sentences crafted for easy and effective delivery, most of the remaining fillers disappeared without direct attention. Every single improvement to your delivery skills has a much greater effect than you might imagine.

DELIVERY TIPS TO HELP YOU CONNECT DURING YOUR SPEECH

With a confident, energetic delivery and a focus on your audience, you've created a positive impression with your opening. By now the worst of your anxiety has likely abated,[6] and so you need only use a variety of delivery techniques to enhance your message and help your audience stay attentive. In this section, I'll give you a few ideas for adding variety to your delivery style.

Eye Contact

In the opening you used a great deal of eye contact, and you might have focused it on a few, supportive people. In the body of the speech, you'll need to include additional members of the audience. Use strong sustained eye contact with someone in your audience as you conclude each point, let your eyes move more quickly through the audience between points, look down, or at your visual, and then back to someone in your audience to begin your next point.

You can also use your eyes to add expression to your message. Let them roll to suggest disbelief, wink slightly to signal a shared bit of humour, open them widely with raised eyebrows to suggest surprise, and wince and close your eyes briefly to indicate a painful question or message. Don't overdo these theatrics. They can be used in any setting but must be appropriate to the topic and audience. Tone them down for a boardroom presentation of a serious business proposal and give them full delivery in a large theater setting. Use a mirror or video camera to perfect your expressions and become more lively with your facial movements.

Posture

In the opening you used an energetic, upright posture to signal your confidence. Vary your posture slightly in the body of your speech. For example, you could relax it when telling a story or lean slightly (without slumping) on a table or lectern while explaining a point. Moving towards the theatrics again, if you wanted to reinforce a message of dejection (most likely in a story), you could really let your body slump. Aim for variety since this helps your audience stay attentive.

Movement

To keep your own energy level high, move around periodically during a speech. I don't mean sway or rock in one place, I mean move your feet and change positions. When you move towards your audience, you'll add to the feeling of being comfortable with them, and it is also an excellent way to reinforce the importance of a point. Move towards them as you begin to make the point, but stand still while you actually make it. After emphasizing the point, you can indicate your transition by moving smoothly back to a more central space. Practice this in front of a large window or mirror to learn to control your movement by contrasting vigorous moves with periods of stillness.

Hand Gestures

Use gesture to reinforce your message. An open gesture is one in which the audience sees the palms of your hands, and to some extent, your inner arm. A closed gesture is one in which the audience sees the backs of your hands. The first is friendlier, as if the speaker were totally comfortable, open, and honest with the audience. To fully achieve this effect, you'll need to use relaxed gestures, sustaining them for periods of a second or two rather than hastily jabbing a finger here and a hand there.

Avoid gestures that make listeners feel you are talking down to them. If you think of the gestures your parents, teachers, clergy, or other adult authorities used in scolding you, you'll have a good idea of the kinds of gestures to avoid. The pointed finger is an excellent example of a gesture we associate from childhood with being corrected or scolded. When you use it while speaking to adults, many will subconsciously feel uncomfortable because of the childhood associations of the gesture. Imagine someone talking to you with their hands on their hips. Where did you first see that? Was it a friendly, collegial encounter or was it someone scolding you? Imagine someone talking to you with their arms tightly folded across their chest, body tense, lips tight, and eyes glaring. Is this the image you want to give your listeners? Again, rehearsal in front of a mirror or window will help you remember to adjust your gestures to avoid offending anyone.

Variety Helps

You can help the audience stay attentive and improve your own breathing by using a variety of gestures. These need to be sized to the space you're working in (smaller gestures for a smaller room), but otherwise be assertive and creative in your movements. Let your gestures move away from your body, sustain some, and move others rapidly, have some asymmetrical and others symmetrical, use your whole arm and upper body for some, use only finger tips or hand and wrist for others. It is the variety rather than any single gesture that energizes you and your audience.

Too much gesture or non-stop gesture serves only to distract and irritate, so you also need to become comfortable with your hands resting still at your sides. Try to break the habit of keeping them clutched in front of your body or behind your back. These positions are closed, encourage slumped posture, and make it harder to get your hands active again. Leaving your hands at your sides allows you to maintain good posture without seeming stiff and readies your hands for their next vivid gesture.

Vocal improvements

Variety is the key to body language and also to your success vocally. Fortunately, when you use upright posture and lively body language, your breathing is good and you are more expressive vocally without any additional effort.

Dialogue

To add more variety to your vocal repertoire, incorporate dialogue. *"Many of you have asked me, 'How can we get customers to pay more for what seems like less?' And I've been telling you, 'You have to show them it isn't really less!' In the next segment...."* If you read this example with expression, you will notice the opportunity afforded by the use of dialogue. Even in the most serious business presentation or conference speech, you can inject a change of pace through dialogue.

Style

Use a variety of voice levels and styles. Even in a business presentation, soften your voice now and then. A softer voice is often useful for examples while a louder, crisper style suits the delivery of stark facts. Add a lively conversational style for even more variety. It suits the portions of a speech where you help your audience connect with your material. Rather than, *"this is important because..."* you could say, *"Now you might be wondering, how is this important to me? Why is Marg telling me this right now? The answer is easy. You're going to be a world-class speaker and world-class speakers connect with their listeners."*

Pace

Vary the pace of your speech and the duration of the pauses. Speed up for stories and examples, when reviewing known material, or leading them through simple background material. Slow down for key ideas and use pauses to give emphasis to each important point.

The language of speech

Formality

Mix your formal language and expression with occasional informal or street expressions. In a speech about advanced air traffic control systems, an engineer drew mild laughter and stimulated attention when, after listing all the challenges they were facing in their software development, said, *"Well — gee whiz! When I listen to this list I wonder why I get up in the morning."* Later in the speech, right in the middle of discussing a client's concerns he said, *"You know, I realized they (the client) were right. And boy, that frosted my socks!"* Those informal expressions worked into an otherwise technical speech added a little sparkle to help draw audience attention and create the bond of shared frustration.

Fillers

Use a tape recorder or a partner to help identify any words or sounds you use excessively. Expressions such as *you know, basically, essentially, okay*, and *clearly* are often overused as are cliché expressions such as *last but not least* and *without further ado*. Filler words and sounds *(um, ah, eh, huh?, and-uh, so-oh)* also creep into speeches, and if used frequently, deter listening. Once you determine which words and sounds you rely on, you can seek to eliminate those that aren't productive and reduce the use of others by finding alternatives.

Delivery, as you have seen in this chapter, is more than simply your ability to display marvellous posture and incorporate perfect gestures. Delivery is about how you appear, sound, and behave from the first moments of your arrival to the time you leave the setting. How you act before, during and after your speech are sometimes more important than the content of the speech itself.

SUMMARY: USE YOUR DELIVERY SKILLS TO ENHANCE THE CONNECTION

- Use sustained eye contact to connect visually with listeners.
- Look at your audience while you finish each key point, and then relax your focus to let them absorb your message.
- Choose an upright, energetic posture, and then vary it slightly when appropriate to your message.
- Move deliberately; remain still at times for contrast and emphasis.
- Add a variety of open, sustained gestures.
- Avoid gestures such as the pointed finger, arms akimbo, and hands on hips because of their effect of distancing you from your audience.
- Rehearse in front of the mirror or a window to improve posture, gesture, and movement.

- Add vocal variety, but don't become overly theatrical unless a very large audience or the topic (entertainment, motivational) demands it.

- Use an audio tape to discover filler sounds, overused words and phrases, repetitive rhythms or pitch patterns, and lengthy phrases.

Notes

1 Remote amplification works well in most situations. The speaker wears a very small lapel microphone with a short wire leading to a light battery pack clipped on a waistband or belt. The battery pack, about the size of a pager or garage door opener, transmits to a remote receiver and from there sound is amplified through a normal sound system.

2 To get an idea of your gesture, posture, and movement select a large window. Work with the lights on inside when it's dark or dusky outside. The window provides a large screen for you to observe your movements. You can also use a mirror, although being smaller they tend to limit your movement and give too much detail. The audience is rarely close enough to see a slight blemish on your forehead but you'll see it in the mirror.

3 Fig-leaf position – hands clasped or resting over genitalia. This is a closed posture that frequently limits gesture and encourages a slumped posture.

4 Pitching-up – or raising the pitch of the voice is common when asking a question in English. *"Have any of you ever wanted to lose weight?"* would sound natural if the speaker raised the pitch of her voice as she neared the end of the sentence. The change in pitch signals the desire for some sort of response. Pitching-up when making a statement such as, *"My department can help you establish a realistic goal.",* sounds as if the speaker wasn't quite sure and was asking the audience to confirm it. The overall result is usually not very positive with the audience feeling the speaker's lack of confidence and conviction.

5 *"Okay?"* used at the end of a sentence is an example of a *tag question*. Used infrequently, tag questions check for audience agreement, but if used excessively, they are irritating. Speakers who use excessive tag questions give the impression they lack confidence in their remarks and need the listeners approval or agreement to continue speaking.

6 Most speakers find their anxiety is worst just before and in the early minutes of a speech. There are speakers who are fine when they start but are prone to panic attacks five to ten minutes into a speech. This is rare amongst speakers who are very focused on their audience because by then they can tell the audience is with them, interested and focused.

CHAPTER 15

CLOSE AND CONNECT

You've won and held their attention, you've made your points but now it's time to close the speech and get the action you want. In many cases it's time to handle questions and mingle with your audience. You have many additional opportunities to influence and win the support of your listeners if you continue your effort through the following segments of your speech or presentation.

YOUR CLOSING REMARKS

I've seen few speakers who could save a dreadful speech in the last dying moments, but I've seen many good speakers who, after connecting throughout their speeches, lost momentum and impact in their closing. Sometimes the content was right but the delivery wasn't, sometimes the delivery was there but the speaker didn't say anything of value, and in the worst cases, there was no delivery and no conclusion; the speaker just ran out of steam.

At the end of your speech, think of yourself like a sales professional closing the sale. Your entire attention is focused on your customers, your enthusiasm or deep belief is obvious, and your remarks are reminders of what has been said and why they should buy. As you close, ask your audience to buy and tell them how to act or think or feel. At the end of most speeches, you'll want to include most of the following items:

A review of what you've covered. In the opening you previewed the topics you'd cover. The review covers the same material but is delivered in past tense.

A reminder of *why* they should care, or why this matters to them.

Again, this material was already developed for your opening. Often a story or example can be used at this stage to bring emotional impact to the conclusion.

A call for action. *"Please join me this Saturday to begin clean-up of the Passion Creek Canyon area."* Tell your audience what you want them to do, think, or feel. In a motivational or inspirational message, you might not be so overt in your request for action. You could use an indirect sales statement or even a question. *"It's your life. Will it be a life of service? Will it be a life others remember with admiration, love, and respect? Will it be a life you can feel proud of? The choice is yours!"*

A full stop. Let your audience know you are finished.

DELIVERY COUNTS IN YOUR CLOSING COMMENTS

Content is important, but again, how you deliver this message is as important as what you say. If you mumble through your closing remarks, rush through them at breakneck pace, or deliver them blithely as if they were a bit embarrassing or unimportant, even the best content won't have the desired impact. Try these delivery skills for maximum impact:

Slow your pace and increase your pauses so they know you are nearing the end. Separate each point in your summary with a full pause and use an even longer pause before you launch into your conclusion.

Deliver the final words of your speech in a deliberate, slow manner, but don't lose volume. If your voice trails off at the end, your audience will tend to quit listening and mentally move onto the next item on their day's agenda.

Look at the audience as you close. After you finish, maintain eye contact for long enough to let it sink in, and then lower your gaze.

This slight bowing of head and eyes will usually result in applause. In situations where applause is inappropriate, you might want to yield control to someone else by looking right at that person and calling him by name, *"Mr. Blake...."*

If you happen to get thunderous applause or a standing ovation, remain facing the audience and look very pleased. I've periodically seen an otherwise successful speaker dash off stage or out of the speaking position while the applause was still great, and I've thought it a shame. Here was an audience reaching out to indicate their approval and pleasure, only to have the speaker run away from the compliment. Remain standing there, and when the applause dwindles, thank them for their enthusiastic response and perhaps offer to take questions.

No matter how disappointed you are with your own performance, save your self-evaluation for a private place removed from your audience. On occasion, I've seen speakers who I thought did a credible job suddenly slump and shuffle away from the speaking area, quietly admonishing themselves for some imagined transgression. Some looked at their audience and grimaced their self-evaluation, while others closed their eyes and looked away. In each case, I found myself wondering if they'd given us bad information or if they didn't really believe what they'd been saying. Don't break whatever connection you've created, by verbally or non-verbally telling your audience you don't like what you've just done. End with dignity and self-respect.

INVITE THEIR QUESTIONS AND CONNECT

I've often watched speakers who were stiff and mechanical, and who hated giving speeches and presentations, suddenly come alive in a question period. Why? Because they could no longer rely on script, visuals, or outline to distance themselves from their audience. Suddenly they saw individuals, conversed easily with them, and felt the pleasure of connecting.

Speeches don't always include an opportunity for audience questions, but if you've given information, expressed your opinion, or discussed ideas, they seem a logical part of the presentation. Questions are generally a compliment because they indicate your audience was attentive and interested in your material. They indicate you've connected with your listeners, and they give you additional opportunities to connect.

EVEN HOSTILE QUESTIONS CAN BE A SIGN YOU'VE CONNECTED

Occasionally questions can be hostile or challenging, but even this is somewhat positive; it's better to hear all objections and be given an opportunity to respond than to have your audience leave and discredit you later behind your back. Besides, even a negative reaction is a sign you've connected to some extent. I've seen speakers who raised the ire of some members of the audience during their prepared presentation, yet hardly knew it because of their mechanical attention to structure and message. But, when they invited questions and the audience erupted with challenges and disagreement, these same speakers restated, reviewed, supported their earlier contentions, and gradually won the grudging support of their listeners. What began as a barrage of strong negative feelings was converted to a positive connection.

DECIDE WHEN TO TAKE QUESTIONS

You can take questions throughout your presentation so participants can interact with you as they need to, or you can save them for set question periods. Encouraging questions throughout your speech usually provides greater satisfaction for both speaker and audience because the interaction helps both parties get what they need. Early questions give your listeners a chance to let you know what interests them and the areas where they might need more or less information, to follow your presentation. You can learn names, pertinent information and possibly identify participants who have expertise on your topic. Those early questions give your listeners the feeling their needs will be met. They get answers when they need them and don't have to try and remember what question they'd wanted to ask earlier.

Some speakers prefer to take questions only at the end or at set points in a speech. This usually saves some time as questions that might have been asked earlier are now forgotten. It helps speakers who might otherwise get lost or have difficulty bridging back into their planned remarks. With large audiences it is often the best way to deal with question-taking.

MANAGING QUESTIONS EASILY HELPS YOU CONNECT

In this section, I'll offer you ideas for managing the audience through their questions. For a very thorough guide to the types of questions you could be asked and ways to respond to them, read Malcolm Kushner's book, *Successful Presentations for Dummies*.[1] Delivery skills for handling questions are covered in the next part of this chapter.

Assuming your speech isn't an amusing after-dinner speech on polite ways to eat pasta or the eulogy for your favourite lawyer, always offer to handle questions if time permits. If it doesn't, you can offer to remain after the session or suggest alternate ways they may contact you. Give them an e-mail address, phone, or facsimile number and welcome their questions.

PRIME THE PUMP

If you'd like questions throughout your presentation, you'll need to invite this audience response in your opening remarks. Alternately, you can have your introducer tell the audience you'll take questions throughout your speech. You can tease an audience into asking questions by periodically reminding them that you like questions or offering a question yourself. *"A question I'm often asked at this point in my speech is.... Since you haven't asked me any questions yet, would you like me to answer that one?"* You'll only need to do this once and your audience will start to participate.

Another way to prime the pump and get them asking questions is to turn the table. *"Since you aren't asking me any questions, let me ask you one."* Of course you must have a question, preferably one that is interesting to the group and that will stimulate discussion and present useful information.

Once stimulated to ask questions, most groups will continue to do so on their own. Now your challenges could range from managing too many requests to keeping questions on topic. You could be faced with a participant who has difficulty asking a question or one who is belligerent. Your challenge is to remain in control, pleasant and welcoming, but not to let any individual, no matter how entertaining or knowledgeable, dominate the interaction. If you use eye contact, movement, and gesture as recommended in the previous chapter on delivery skills, you shouldn't have much problem, but let's examine a few of the most common situations that arise.

MANAGE THE TRAFFIC

If you suddenly have hands waving in every corner of your room, you'll need to manage the traffic. You'll want to move it around so participants in all areas of the room feel they have equal opportunity, and you'll want to assure participants they will get to ask their questions. First let them know your intent by looking throughout the room, acknowledging the participants' raised hands, and then telling them you'll get to each of them. Now select one participant, succinctly respond, and then select the next participant from another area of the room.

Encourage your audience to listen to each other, *"just in case someone asks the very question you planned to ask,"* but if you do get a duplication of questions, answer very briefly without drawing attention to the duplication. You win no friends by pointing out this lapse of listening skills and risk embarrassing the person who asked.

Suppose a gentleman in your audience asks a convoluted question. He gives you a couple of examples and changes direction frequently. Although you'd like clarification of his question, you can see the audience is growing impatient. First, ask his name. You could simply refer to him as *sir* or *this gentleman* but you'll have more control if you learn and use his name. Let's suppose he told you his name is Joe, you might now say, *"Thank you, Joe. You've asked a complex question. I will summarize it and give you a brief answer."* Your audience will know you understand the problem and plan to manage it. They'll appreciate your efforts, and because you haven't made Joe uncomfortable, they'll support your approach.

Next you restate Joe's question, answer it appropriately, and then encourage others, not Joe, to ask the next question. There will usually be a few members of your audience who will rescue you by asking a question. They don't want to hear more from Joe anymore than you do.

DIFFICULT QUESTIONS AND DIFFICULT PEOPLE

Follow the same basic pattern for someone who is belligerent or rude. It's hard to see this as an opportunity to connect with your audience, yet it truly is. As long as you respond politely to your attacker, your audience will support you. You can try reframing the question or statement, *"I found your suggestions for cleaning Passion Creek Canyon simplistic to the point of ridiculous. Do you really expect us to crawl about the canyon picking up used condoms?"* When you reframe, you restate the question but remove all hostile or rude language so it might become, *"I believe Joe is asking if ordinary citizens, like us, can make a difference in the canyon. The answer is yes!"* This gives you and your audience a chance to hear the question without the emotional overtones. They'll appreciate your maturity and leadership.

In a small group, assuming you'd be willing to handle the emotional response, you can address the feelings in the message and ignore the content, *"You sound really angry, Joe. Is there something else going on here that I should know about?"* Joe may well deny there was any intent to attack, and since you've served him notice, albeit politely, he likely won't try again. There is also a chance you'll escalate the emotions using this technique, but it will give you an opportunity to clear the air and get to the heart of the matter. Your emotional honesty might also help you connect and strengthen the bond with your audience.

In a large group you might want to put it directly (and forcefully) to the audience. *"I think Joe is asking me to defend about two years of committee decisions. This would use a lot of our time. How are the rest of you feeling? Would you like me to go into our decisions in depth or carry on? I could always meet with those of you who are most interested at a later time."* Usually your audience will side with you and encourage you to ignore further requests from Joe.

If you make the mistake of attacking Joe in any way, your audience will turn on you and any goodwill you created will come undone. Controlling your own emotions and connecting with the others in your audience will ensure a successful presentation. I'm amazed by how often others in the audience appreciate a speaker's ability to manage difficult people. I'm also surprised by the number of seemingly hostile participants who, realizing they aren't getting the attention they want by being negative, re-evaluate their position and become friendly supporters. Enjoy this shift, however shallow or transparent it might seem, because you are still on show even after the question period ends.

WHAT IF I DON'T KNOW THE ANSWER?

Speakers often worry about having an answer for every question. You needn't have an answer, and if you don't, it's better to be honest about it. Sometimes the person asking already knows the answer and will provide it if prompted, sometimes another audience member can supply an adequate answer, sometimes you can offer to contact the questioner after you've had time to check your facts, and sometimes you'll simply want to declare the question as beyond the limits of the topic under discussion. Even if you don't know the answer, you still need to have an adequate response and to stay in control.

Sometimes the question is beyond the scope of your expertise. You can simply say, *"I'm not an expert on that. Would anyone else like to respond?"* Sometimes the person who asked the question already knew the answer and was trying to trip you up. Far better to share the stage briefly with the show-off than risk a showdown by giving false information.

Sometimes the question would be better answered by someone else in the meeting room. Perhaps the question is financial and Agnes, your chief financial officer, is present. Although you might stumble through the answer if she wasn't present, why not invite her to participate? *"Agnes is really our expert on that. Would you mind explaining it for us, Agnes?"* She'll probably be delighted to assist you, but if she demurs you could say, *"Well then, I'll give it a try, but if you hear me making any errors, Agnes, please correct me."*

If you should know the answer, or you can get the answer, you could say, *"I can't give you a precise answer now, but I will get that information for you."* In a speech before a large audience, ask the questioner to write the question on his or her business card and leave it with you after the speech. With a small group, such as you'd have in a proposal to decision-makers, you'll need to remember who asked. Either way you can follow up with your questioner and no harm is done. In fact, you'll have an excuse to contact them again, and this provides one more opportunity to win their support and appreciation.

Having a response is important, but delivering with dignity is equally important when fielding questions. The following section offers some general tips on using your delivery skills to connect when taking questions.

DELIVERY TIPS TO HELP YOU CONNECT WHEN HANDLING QUESTIONS

Although I've touched on some of these suggestions in the previous section because they are so useful in stimulating and managing questions, the following tips will give additional detail on using a powerful delivery to enhance your question period. Consider them as suggestions and think of your own situation before incorporating each.

- Welcome questions by moving towards your audience and opening your hands and arms towards them. Smile and look at your listeners. Using open and welcoming body language reinforces the message that you look forward to their questions.

- When you welcome questions, you might have to wait a bit for them. Look at your audience during this time. Smile or look thoughtful. Your attention suggests you really do want to hear their questions.

- When someone does ask a question, give them your full attention.

- If you need a moment to think, acknowledge the question, and then look down briefly. Watch someone else do this and you'll notice how thoughtful they appear. If a speaker gazes out the window or up at the heavens, you're more likely to think that person is desperate.

Make sure you understand the question and paraphrase it if you feel your listeners might not have heard it. If your speech is being taped, restate the questions so anyone listening to the tape later will know what question you are answering.

Respond succinctly. If the answer will be lengthy, you could ask the audience if they'd be willing to entertain it, or you could offer to meet afterwards with those who are interested.

As you respond, move your eye contact to include individuals throughout the meeting room. You are answering one person's question, but you don't want to end up in a dialogue with that individual. You still want to connect with your entire audience.

Warn the audience when you are nearly out of time, and if there are residual questions, offer to remain afterwards to answer them.

If, as you read the preceding list of techniques, you thought of a situation where you wouldn't do what I've suggested, don't be surprised. No technique works perfectly in every situation and a speaker must choose wisely. Sometimes you should avoid a technique suggested here. A good example was given to me by a young woman of Chinese descent. She spoke to a local Chinese benevolent organization comprised mainly of older Chinese men. Raised in China and Hong Kong, they were accustomed to traditional body language. After her first presentation, her uncle, a member of the organization, patiently explained that she must not look directly into the eyes of the men. Her direct eye contact, so useful in her normal business life, made them feel very uncomfortable. Once she adjusted her eye contact, they responded favourably to her requests for funding various community projects.

From this example, you can see how there really are very few rules for speakers. You must always be asking yourself *why* you are choosing a particular technique or approach. Every choice you make will impact your ability to connect with the listener and therefore your ability to communicate your message.

AFTER YOUR SPEECH – KEEP ON CONNECTING

The speaker was a medical doctor discussing ways to increase communication with patients. He'd spoken about sitting down to talk to patients and mentioned how it improved the relationship with them and coincidentally improved a doctor's listening skills. I was captivated with his remarks and some research studies he discussed. As he finished talking he was already dismantling his slides, and when I approached he turned away from me. I could see he was busy so I waited patiently. He talked to the woman who'd introduced him but did not seem interested in talking to me. The rest of the participants were waiting in line for the buffet lunch, so once he'd gathered his materials I was reasonably sure he'd have a moment to talk with me. Finally, when he'd packed up everything, I spoke up, introduced myself, and asked about his research. He said, *"Can't you see I'm busy right now?"* and once again turned away. Was the research fictitious, was he a fraud or simply an unfriendly speaker? Moments before, excited about the information he'd discussed, I'd been ready to suggest him as a speaker at an upcoming conference, and now I was disgusted.

You've finished your speech, you've handled questions, perhaps someone has thanked you, and now you might believe your performance is finished. In most cases you'd be wrong. When you've connected with an audience, one of your greatest opportunities for reinforcing the message and your relationship occurs once the formal program has ended. Professional speakers meet their audiences to accept accolades but also to sign books, sell audio and visual products, meet potential clients, distribute marketing materials, and answer additional questions. Business speakers use the time to handle objections, re-sell the concepts of their presentations, and get feedback. Again, your behaviour can greatly influence the feelings you generate in your audience.

- Be visible and accessible. Sometimes you can remain on the stage area or at the front of the room, but if someone else needs that space consider moving near the door where your audience will exit or to the refreshment area.

- Use your best networking skills to meet and greet your admirers. Smile, make eye contact, shake hands, and learn their names. Ask for their business cards and offer yours. This is your opportunity to close the sale personally.

- Graciously thank them for accolades and be equally gracious about suggestions for improvement. Even if you wouldn't think of changing anything, you can say, *"I appreciate your suggestion,"* or, *"You've raised an interesting point. I want to think about that."* I've gained some valuable ideas from some very clumsy evaluations delivered while others waited to talk to me.

If there are others waiting, keep your discussions brief and offer a follow-up meeting or mailing if it seems appropriate. Most participants will be quite considerate of you and the others waiting to meet you, but if you have someone who isn't good at picking up the social cues, you can end your visit by saying something like, *"Joe, I've really enjoyed talking to you. Good luck with your first aid training school."* Shake Joe's hand again and then look past him to the next person waiting to speak with you. Greet this person and don't look back at Joe.

If you must pack up while talking to audience members, apologize for doing two things at once or deputize them to assist you.

If you need to leave to catch a plane or for some other essential deadline, warn those awaiting your attention. You can suggest they leave you a business card and write their message, question, or request on the back so you can get back to them later.

If your speech was hosted, contact your host(s) following the session to convey your thanks for their care and kindness. A phone call or facsimile message is adequate although a personal note is often more memorable and suggests extra effort.

As you can see, your speech isn't over until you are clear of the building and area where you gave it. Early in my career I took a week-long speaking engagement at a company retreat. Although I spoke for only about three hours each day, I knew I was, at least technically, still on stage. If I was grabbing breakfast in the coffee shop, one or more of the participants would inevitably join me for informal discussion. When I was resting on the beach, participants would drop by to discuss ideas and ask advice. Even when they partied in the evenings, I never felt entirely off-duty so I kept my evenings short and avoided alcohol. The last night we had a blowout party, and I finally relaxed with a bit of the grape.

When the vice-president gave his final speech of the evening, I was only partially attentive. Moments after he finished, he paid me the great compliment of asking my opinion of his speech. I wasn't able to give him a credible evaluation, but I did learn my lesson. As long as you're with an audience or client group, you are performing and must never forget it.

Summary: Close and Connect

- Close your speech with energy and dignity.
- Include a review of your main points and ask for action.
- Boldly invite questions and await audience response.
- Use each question to reinforce your main points and further connect with your audience.
- Stay in control even when questions are long, challenging, or rude – your audience will appreciate your leadership.
- Use eye contact, upright posture, open gestures, and a vigorous style to keep the question period engaging and lively.
- After your speech keep the connection going with those who come to speak to you.
- Follow your presentation with a message of thanks to those who supported your efforts.

Notes

1 Kushner, Malcolm. *Successful Presentations For Dummies*. IDG Books Worldwide, Foster City, CA, 1996.

CHAPTER 16

CONNECT TO COMMUNICATE

We all need to communicate. We need to express our ideas and feel we've been heard. We need to influence others. Without any training, an infant uses crying combined with body language to influence parents or other caregivers to provide the love and sustenance required for survival. As we mature we increase our communication repertoire to include specific words and actions, thus improving our ability to influence others and broadening the sophistication of our manipulative abilities. Through observation and experimentation, we continue to refine our ability to have an effect on others.

Presentations and public speaking require the strategic and refined application of the skills developed throughout our lives. We seek to understand the audience, to gauge listener response, to adjust message and delivery, and so to engage in real communication rather than simply talking at an assembly or getting through some planned remarks. Through our speeches we want to change attitudes, beliefs, actions, and ideas. To influence others in this way we must connect, in every way possible, with our listeners.

I have urged you to think of your presentations and speeches as an interactive experience. I have urged you to avoid rules, to stop thinking there is a right way or a best way to accomplish your communication, but instead to become ever more vigilant in making choices about how you communicate. I have encouraged you to place your primary focus on others, rather than on yourself and to engage in audience analysis throughout the planning, delivery, and follow-up of your speech or presentation.

The results of this audience-focused approach are startling. Your audiences will be more attentive and interested. They'll retain more of your message and take the actions you recommend. Not only will audiences appreciate your efforts to connect, but you'll discover speaking is a pleasurable and rewarding activity. You'll then seek more opportunities to speak to groups which is good for your career and provides additional practice.

The best speakers I've ever heard were not those who had the best speechwriters or were even the most intellectually capable. They didn't spend the most time creating or rehearsing their speeches, and they didn't spend the most money on elaborate visual aids. Interestingly, they still felt anxious or excited before an important speech, and they still worried about the details of what they'd say and how it would sound. They didn't have an identical strategy for preparing speeches, and they didn't even use the same techniques in every speech. But, as I observed and interviewed the best speakers, I did identify one commonality that distinguished them from the many speakers who were just going through the motions – they had a strong audience focus.

The best speakers I've heard cared deeply about their audiences. No matter how large the group or how difficult the situation, they made me feel they were talking to me. They had done their home-work in evaluating the audience, and they had created a flexible plan that allowed for adjustment throughout the communication process. They had infused their speeches with stories, examples, humour, visual support, and interaction and provided strong connections and opportunities to observe our responses. Their delivery skills supported and enhanced the connections. And, when something went wrong, whether it was a participant who reacted badly or a situation beyond the control of any individual in the room, the best speakers rose to the occasion and strengthened the connection through their audience-focused response to the situation.

You can connect through your speeches and presentations. You might have to give up some long-cherished ideas about the correct way to speak to groups. You might have to adjust your focus or alter your speaking style slightly. But I believe the rewards are worth it. When you truly connect and feel that connection, you will distinguish yourself amongst speakers and you will experience an energy and excitement you've never felt before. Keep speaking, keep practicing, and above all, keep connecting - for that is the essence of communication.

MARGARET GREW UP IN THE RURAL NORTH OKANAGAN REGION OF British Columbia. She began public speaking through her participation in 4H competitions. After completing a degree in Physical Education at the University of Calgary (B.P.E. with Distinction, 1973) and teacher education at Simon Fraser University (P.D.P., 1974), she worked for six years in public education. In 1975, she joined Toastmasters and soon began teaching adult education courses and creating communications seminars for school administrators.

Returning to Simon Fraser University, she completed a Masters degree (M.Ed., 1984) focusing on how to best help adolescents and adults become more comfortable and effective as speakers. She was soon offered teaching opportunities at two universities and from that experience created her own business, Lions Gate Training Ltd.

Through her company, Margaret offers fully customized communications training programs on topics ranging from public speaking and instructional presentations to interpersonal communication and business networking. She also offers private coaching for those who want to improve their speaking skills. Many clients come to her when faced with the challenge of a specific presentation, a job interview, or a difficult communication situation. Others come for general improvement because they know their career and business success depends on strong, professional communication skills.

Increasingly, Margaret has been performing at conferences and meetings as a keynote speaker and workshop leader. While communication is always part of her message, audiences also appreciate her ability to entertain and motivate. Clients rave about her willingness to create programs designed just for them.

In 1995, after completing an arduous qualification process and performing before an international panel of adjudicators, Margaret was recognized as an Accredited Professional Speaker. This recognition has been given to only 46 speakers worldwide since Toastmasters International began the Accredited Speaker program in 1980.

The following year, Rotary International recognized Margaret as a Paul Harris Fellow, an award honouring her work as a volunteer. Her volunteer activities include work with Rotary, 4H, Girl Guides of Canada, Junior League, and many other organizations.

Margaret is married to an entrepreneur and garden railroad fanatic. Together they share a passion for travel. The Galapagos Islands and Vietnam remain her favourite travel experiences - but then, she hasn't been everywhere yet.

For further information contact:

Lions Gate Training Ltd.
mhope@lionsgate.ca
www.lionsgatetraining.com